Advance praise for
Praying the Rosary Like Never Before

The rosary is meant to be a simple prayer. A simple way to pray that has been available to Christians for hundreds of years. And yet many people are intimidated by this simple prayer. Dr. Sri has written this book to reconnect Catholics with their inheritance given to them in the rosary. This book can help the most inexperienced beginner or the most regular pray-er of the rosary deepen their understanding and experience of this great gift.

—Fr. Michael Schmitz, speaker, and director of youth ministry, Diocese of Duluth

"As we celebrate the one hundredth anniversary of Our Lady's apparitions at Fatima, we remember her timeless message, repeated over and over, to pray the rosary daily. *Praying the Rosary Like Never Before* is an excellent resource for anyone wanting to delve into one of the richest devotions given to us from heaven!"

—Curtis Martin, cofounder of FOCUS, vocation director, Archdiocese of St. Louis

"Dr. Sri's scholarship on Our Lady is tremendous, but his love for her is still deeper. When these two qualities are merged, the result is persuasive and powerful. Whether you love the rosary or have never felt drawn to it, this book will indeed help you to pray it like never before."

—Jason Evert, author,
Saint John Paul the Great: His Five Loves

"Get ready to experience the rosary like never before! Dr. Edward Sri combines intellectual arguments with contemplative inspiration to help us see this age-old prayer in a completely new light. I have no doubt that this book will transform a lot of people's spiritual lives."

—Jennifer Fulwiler, SiriusXM radio host
and author, *Something Other Than God*

Praying the Rosary Like Never Before

Encounter the Wonder of Heaven and Earth

Edward Sri

servant

AN IMPRINT OF
FRANCISCAN MEDIA
Cincinnati, Ohio

Portions of this work were originally published in *The New Rosary in Scripture: Biblical Insights for Praying the Twenty Mysteries* by Dr. Edward Sri (Servant, 2003). Scripture passages have been taken from the *Revised Standard Version*, Catholic edition. Copyright 1946, 1952, 1971 by the Division of Christian Education of the National Council of Churches of Christ in the USA. Used by permission. All rights reserved. Excerpts from the English translation of the *Catechism of the Catholic Church* for use in the United States of America (indicated as *CCC*), 2nd ed. Copyright 1997 by United States Catholic Conference—Libreria Editrice Vaticana. Quotes from John Paul II, Apostolic Letter on the Most Holy Rosary, *Rosarium Virginis Mariae* (indicated as *RVM*), October 16, 2002, are from the Vatican website, www.vatican.va.

Library of Congress Cataloging-in-Publication Data
Names: Sri, Edward P., author.
Title: Praying the rosary like never before / Edward Sri.
Description: Cincinnati : Servant, 2017. | Includes bibliographical references and index.
Identifiers: LCCN 2017021357 | ISBN 9781632531780 (trade paper : alk. paper)
Subjects: LCSH: Rosary. | Prayer—Catholic Church.
Classification: LCC BX2163 .S655 2017 | DDC 242/.74—dc23
LC record available at https://lccn.loc.gov/2017021357

ISBN 978-1-63253-178-0

Copyright ©2017, 2003 Edward Sri. All rights reserved.
Published by Servant, an imprint of
Franciscan Media
28 W. Liberty St.
Cincinnati, OH 45202
www.FranciscanMedia.org

Printed in the United States of America.
Printed on acid-free paper.
17 18 19 20 21 5 4 3

To my daughter
Madeleine

These words express, so to speak, *the wonder of heaven and earth*; they could be said to give a glimpse of God's own wonderment as he contemplates his "masterpiece"—the Incarnation of the Son in the womb of the Virgin Mary.... The repetition of the Hail Mary in the Rosary gives us a share in God's own wonder and pleasure: In jubilant amazement we acknowledge the greatest miracle of history.

—Pope St. John Paul II

CONTENTS

*E*ncounter *the Wonder of Heaven and Earth* is, no doubt, a surprising subtitle for a book on the rosary. While I've certainly met people who say they love the rosary and find it easy, comforting, and even exhilarating to pray, I've met countless more—young and old, laity and clergy—who experience the rosary with anything but awe and wonder. Words such as *long, boring, difficult,* and *old-fashioned* are more likely to describe their impressions of this powerful devotion.

Maybe you've been there. Maybe you are one of the many Catholics who have tremendous respect for the rosary but struggle in praying it. You get distracted. You get bored. You prefer other forms of prayer.

Or perhaps you resonate with those who say they don't get much out of the rosary. It feels too mechanical. Does repeating all these words really make a difference? Maybe you are one of the many young adult Catholics who think of the rosary as something their grandmother prays or as the funeral home prayer—not a devotion that speaks to our lives today. Or maybe you identify with those who sincerely would like to pray the rosary but can't find time to do it. It takes too long.

A good Catholic friend of mine summed up what I think is the sentiment of many: "If you could help a simple, ordinary guy like me understand what the rosary is all about and inspire me to find time to pray it, that would go a long way. *I just need to figure out how to pray it in a way that will be meaningful to me.*"

That's what this book aims to do: inspire ordinary Catholics to turn to their beads more often and help them pray the rosary in a way that is meaningful for their lives—in a way that is truly life-giving. And in the process, I hope they'll discover what many great saints and ordinary folk throughout the centuries have experienced: a deeper peace, joy, and encouragement that comes from the subtle but profound encounter one can have with Jesus and Mary in this prayer.

Indeed, when prayed with the wisdom of its tradition, the rosary is anything but rote prayer. The Church offers practical insights to enable us to enter more profoundly, and from the depths of our hearts, into what St. John Paul II called the "wonder of heaven and earth" over the mystery of Christ that every Hail Mary in the rosary is meant to express (*RVM*, 33).[1]

This work is different from other rosary books in that it seeks to meet people where they are. I don't aim just to celebrate the glories of the rosary but also to address people's real felt needs with this devotion: their struggles in praying it, their wandering minds, their difficulties in finding time for it. This book also considers common questions people have about the rosary, such as the significance of the Hail Mary, whether the attention given to Mary distracts us from God, the meaning of all the repetition, where the rosary came from, what to think about for each of the mysteries, and whether one should focus on the prayers or the mysteries.

This book also seeks to provide a variety of practical ways to pray the rosary—suggestions that come from the rosary's tradition and, most especially, St. John Paul II. These are helpful tips that we can incorporate in the different seasons, moments, and challenges we face in our lives. These tips can benefit beginners, serving as easy on-ramps for those who don't pray the rosary regularly. And they can motivate avid devotees of the rosary to go deeper with the Lord in this devotion.

Praying the Rosary Like Never Before is based on my 2003 book, *The New Rosary in Scripture*, which was published in the wake of Pope John

Paul II's introduction of the Luminous Mysteries. This new edition significantly reworks much of the original material and includes additional chapters as well as many new insights to help draw people into a richer encounter with God in this prayer. I've also added reflection questions for each chapter, to provide a valuable resource for small group studies.

Through Our Lady's intercession, I pray that that this book will be a helpful introduction for beginners, an inspiration for those who don't pray the rosary as regularly as they'd like, and a helpful guide for those hungering to go deeper with Jesus and Mary through praying the rosary.

Edward Sri

September 8, 2016

Feast of the Nativity of the Blessed Virgin Mary

CHAPTER ONE

Why Pray the Rosary?

Many great popes, saints, and Christian leaders have exhorted us to pray the rosary. It's a powerful prayer, they say, one that can change your life, strengthen the family, bring peace to the world, convert entire nations, and win the salvation of souls.

But does the average person experience the rosary this way?

Many Catholics, unfortunately, have the impression that the rosary is not relevant for them. It might be a sacred prayer for very religious people—priests, religious sisters, and exceptional Catholics—but not for "an ordinary lay person like me." Even some devout Catholics admit that they are a bit intimidated by this prayer. They have tremendous respect for the rosary, know it's important, but feel bad that they don't love it more. Many view it as the marathon of Catholic devotions. "I know it's an important prayer, but it takes fifteen to twenty minutes. I'm too busy. I don't have time for that." "It's too hard to stay focused for that much time. I prefer shorter prayers."

Some have questions about the rosary: Does all this attention to Mary distract us from a relationship with God? Why do we repeat the same prayers over and over? Are we supposed to concentrate on the prayers, the mysteries, or both? Still others think the rosary is just plain boring—a monotonous, dry, mechanical way of talking to God, not as personal and meaningful as other forms of prayer. "It's like taking the garbage out for your wife. You know you should do it, but date night is more exciting." "Sure, the rosary might be good for you—like flossing your teeth—but it's not as interesting and meaningful to me as spiritual reading or adoration."

Others wonder if all the repetition has any meaning. "I know the rosary is important, but it just seems like rote prayer," one young adult said. "It's like saying magical words and something good is supposed to happen. What's the point? Is simply saying these words actually doing anything for me spiritually?"

But what if I were to show you that there is a lot more going on in the rosary than simply saying these words and counting them with beads? What if I were to tell you that the rosary is not beyond you—that you, wherever you may be in your relationship with God, can actually experience a profound, intimate, personal encounter with Jesus through this devotion? And what if you were to discover that there are many different ways to pray the rosary—indeed, some that can easily fit within your schedule and help you with whatever challenges you face right now in your life.

> "There is a lot more going on in the rosary than 'simply saying these words.'"

Think of the rosary as being like the ocean: There's something in it for everyone, whether you consider yourself a veteran mystic longing to go deeper in prayer with our Lord, a novice struggling to learn how to pray, or someone seeking the Lord's help, right now, with something going on in your life. The deep-sea explorer and the child making sand castles on the beach can fully enjoy the same ocean while playing at different levels. And this is true with the rosary.

GETTING YOUR FEET WET

If the rosary is not a part of your regular prayer life right now, it's easy to get your feet wet with this devotion. Here are five key things you need to know to get started.

First, *we don't have to pray the rosary all at once.* Sure, some people might sit down and quietly pray a whole rosary in one sitting. But we can also choose to divide it up, saying just a decade or two at a time at different points throughout the day: on the way to work, in between errands, in between meetings, while folding laundry or doing dishes. Many holy men and women and even popes have prayed the rosary this way and have found it manageable and fruitful for their busy lives.

Second, *we can pray it anywhere!* The rosary is like a portable chapel we can keep in our pocket and pull out anytime, anyplace. Whether we have a sudden, urgent situation to present to God in prayer or we just want to fill some of our day with thoughts of God, all we need to do is pull out our beads and turn to the Lord in this prayer. Indeed, the rosary is always accessible. We might pray it in a church, in our room, in our office. Or we might pray it in the car, on the exercise machine, in the grocery store line, or while cutting the grass or going for a walk. Bringing our hearts into the rhythm of the rosary is something we can do intermittently throughout the day.

Third, *we can pray the rosary in different ways*, customizing it to fit the needs of the moment. Sometimes we might focus on the words of the prayers, thinking, for example, of Gabriel's greeting to Our Lady as we slowly say with great devotion, "Hail Mary, full of grace, the Lord is with thee." At other times, we might reflect on the mysteries of Christ's life, prayerfully contemplating scenes such as his birth in Bethlehem, his transfiguration, or his death on the cross, etching the Gospel on our hearts. At still other times, we might focus on the holy name of Jesus at the center of each Hail Mary, speaking his name tenderly with love as the pulse of our rosary.

Two and a Half Minutes That Can Change Your Day

Fourth, *it's easy to fit the rosary into your schedule.* Do you have two and a half minutes in your day that you can give to God? This is the beauty of the rosary.

If I need a quick pause in my busy life—just a two-and-a-half-minute break—I can pull out my beads and pray a decade in order to regroup with the Lord and be nourished spiritually. That's all a decade takes: one Our Father, ten Hail Marys, and one Glory Be. I can do that easily, pausing for a moment in between emails, in the car, in my office, in between meetings, in between errands. I don't even have to stop some things I'm doing: I can pray a decade while cooking dinner, sweeping the floor, holding a baby, or walking to my next appointment.

If an urgent need comes up in the day—someone is in an accident, I'm about to begin a big project, my spouse is having a rough day, I have an important decision to make, I need to have a difficult conversation with someone, my child is taking an exam—I can say a quick decade right on the spot. In just two and a half minutes, I can offer a special gift to God—one decade of the rosary—for that particular intention.

Fifth, *even if I'm not able to give the rosary my full attention, it's still worth praying.* I might not always be able to completely unplug mentally from the concerns of the day. I might be exhausted, too tired to pray well. I might be distracted and unable to reach the heights of contemplation. But still, the words themselves are biblical and holy. Offering God a decade or two in the midst of my daily life gives him something beautiful, even if I give it without my full, relaxed, undivided attention. I'm giving God some space in my day and filling it with words of praise for him.

Going Deeper

But the rosary can take us deeper—a lot deeper. When we pray the rosary in its ideal setting, doing a whole set of mysteries, the prayer can slow us down, calm our hearts, and enable us to rest in God's presence. It draws out the deepest desires in our souls, desires for God and God alone.

The rhythm of the repetitious prayers can have a profound spiritual effect. In this, it is much like the traditional "Jesus Prayer" many early Christians recited: "Lord Jesus Christ, Son of God, have mercy on me, a sinner." They would slowly repeat these words over and over again throughout the day, such that the rhythm of this prayer was linked to the rhythm of their breathing. As John Paul II explained, this loving repetition "embodies the desire for Christ to become the breath, soul and all of one's life" (*RVM*, 27). In the same way, the repeated prayers in the rosary help us get more in touch with the deepest desires in our souls for God.

> "The rosary is like a portable chapel we can keep in our pocket and pull out anytime, any place."

We as human persons are made with infinite desires that only God can fulfill. But because we're fallen, we tend to live at the level of our superficial desires—desires for comfort, fun, fame, wealth, pleasure, success. These desires are not bad, but the rosary helps us be more aware of the soul's deepest desires, which are for God. As St. Catherine of Siena taught, the greatest gift we can give to God in prayer is not the finite work of saying the words but our "infinitely desirous love" for God that is expressed in those words and that is being drawn out of our souls in prayer.[1]

How might this happen in the rosary? As we'll see more in chapter 4, when we pray the rosary, we can focus on the name of Jesus at the center of every Hail Mary. We can simply speak Jesus's name with fervent, heartfelt love. We can gather all our desires into that one word, his beautiful, holy name. And with each Hail Mary, we can call out to him, like a lover speaking to the beloved: "Blessed is the fruit of thy womb, *Jesus...Jesus...Jesus.*"

A Spiritual Journey

But that's not all. The rosary also takes us on a profound spiritual journey through the life of Jesus. With each decade (group of ten Hail Marys), we are encouraged to meditate on a different aspect of Jesus's life, from his conception to his public ministry, his passion and death, his resurrection triumph, and beyond (see chapters 8 through 11). In this way, the rosary presents the mysteries of Jesus's life so that we can be ever more conformed to Christ—to think like him, live like him, love like him.

So we don't always have to focus on the words of the Our Father, Hail Mary, and Glory Be. We can simply allow the repetition of the prayers— the "quiet rhythm" and "lingering pace" of the rosary (*RVM*, 12)—to help us slow down, clear our minds, and meditate on the mysteries of Our Lord's life, putting ourselves into the scenes and prayerfully imagining an encounter with Jesus in them.

The Mary Difference

While we can benefit from reflecting on Christ's life in many other settings (whether it be in our own prayer with the Bible, other devotions, and other books and guides), doing so in the rosary comes with a unique benefit. For when we meditate on the mysteries of Christ in the rosary, we do so with the one human person who was closest to Our Lord and contemplated his life most perfectly: the Blessed Virgin Mary. As John Paul II explained, "No one has ever devoted himself to the contemplation of the face of Christ as faithfully as Mary" (*RVM*, 10).

Think about it: From the moment Mary began carrying Jesus in her womb, to his birth, childhood, and upbringing, to his first miracle at Cana and all the way to the cross, she, as his mother, constantly and most ardently contemplated the mystery of her son. Indeed, "Mary lived with her eyes fixed on Christ, treasuring his every word: 'She kept all these things, pondering them in her heart' (Luke 2:19; cf. 2:51)" (*RVM*, 11).

If we want to reflect on Jesus's life—so we can know him, love him, and imitate him more—why wouldn't we want to do this with his mother, Mary? For in the rosary, we "enter into contact with the memories and the contemplative gaze of Mary" (*RVM*, 11). The rosary "mystically transports us to Mary's side as she is busy watching over the human growth of Christ in the home of Nazareth" (*RVM*, 15) so that we can learn from her "to 'read' Christ, to discover his secrets and to understand his message" (*RVM*, 14). As our spiritual mother, Mary is praying for us, helping us notice what Jesus wants us to notice in the mysteries, helping us encounter her son more profoundly than we could on our own.

> "If we want to reflect on Jesus's life, why wouldn't we want to do this with his mother, Mary?"

There is one more reason to encourage you to pray the rosary. It comes from a great hero of the modern age, someone for whom the rosary made a profound difference. In fact, the world may not have ever known this man—indeed, the world may be a very different place today—if it wasn't for his devotion to Jesus and Mary in the rosary. That man is St. John Paul II.

From John Paul II's Heart

Shortly after John Paul II assumed the office of Peter in 1978, he stated that the rosary was his favorite prayer. In his 2002 Apostolic Letter on the Holy Rosary, *Rosarium Virginis Mariae*, he bared a part of his soul as he shared about his devotion to this prayer:

> From my youthful years this prayer has held an important place in my spiritual life.... The Rosary has accompanied me in moments of

joy and in moments of difficulty. To it I have entrusted any number of concerns: in it I have always found comfort. (*RVM*, 2)

To feel the full weight of this statement, we must put these words about *finding comfort in moments of difficulty* within the context of John Paul II's life. Here is a man who lost his mother when he was in third grade; his elder brother, Edmund, when he was twelve; and his father when he was twenty. Karol Wojtyla almost lost his own life during the Nazi occupation of Poland, first when he was struck down by a German truck and again when the Gestapo searched his house while he hid in a basement closet. After working in the underground cultural resistance to the Nazi regime as a layman, he later, as a priest and bishop, openly confronted the many evils of a communist government, which was trying to turn Poland into an atheistic society.

One must think of these and many other trials from the pope's life as part of the background to his words, "The Rosary has accompanied me in moments of joy and in *moments of difficulty*. To it I have entrusted any number of concerns: *in it I have always found comfort.*" These are not the words of an abstract theologian or an out-of-touch pastor who is exhorting us to cling to our beads merely for the sake of saving a pious tradition that he fears is in danger of going out of style. No, these words flow from the heart of a man who has experienced much suffering and hope in times of trial.

When John Paul II assumed the office of Peter in 1978, he entrusted his entire papacy to the "daily rhythm of the Rosary" (*RVM*, 2). This prayer was a tremendous source of strength and guidance for him in the challenges he faced while serving as pope. In *Rosarium Virginis Mariae*, released at the beginning of his twenty-fifth year as pope, he states:

Twenty-five years later, thinking back over the difficulties which have also been part of my exercise of the [papacy], I feel the need to say once more, as a warm invitation to everyone to experience it personally: the Rosary does indeed "mark the rhythm of human life," bringing it into harmony with the "rhythm" of God's own life, in the joyful communion of the Holy Trinity, our life's destiny and deepest longing. (*RVM*, 25)

Here we encounter one of the most remarkable aspects of John Paul II's letter on the rosary: its highly personal tone. This may be the most important context for understanding his urgent plea for Catholics to rediscover the rosary. In times of trouble, John Paul II always turned to the rosary, bringing the drama of his own life into harmony with the life of God. In this letter, he announced a special "Year of the Rosary," calling on all Catholics to renew their devotion to this traditional prayer. Like a good father, he wanted to share with us the spiritual strength and comfort that he found in this prayer.

Today, as we face so many troubles at home and in the world, John Paul II's insights encourage us to do what he always did in times of crisis: turn to Jesus and Mary in the rosary. So whatever challenges we face—whether in our family or at work, in the culture or in our spiritual life—his words continue to exhort us to take up the rosary again and unite our lives with Christ's in this powerful prayer. In the following pages, we will explore his very timely—but what also are sure to be known as timeless—insights on the meaning of the rosary and how we can pray it with greater devotion.

Our next chapter explores the all-too-human realities of praying the rosary—the distraction, boredom, sleepiness, and even dread we sometimes experience with this devotion. "Sometimes I feel I'm not getting anything out of it," many say. "Should I keep praying it then?" In the four chapters that follow, we address common questions people have about Mary and the rosary, such as, "Why do Catholics give so much attention to Mary?" "Why do they pray to her?" "What is the purpose of all the repetitious prayer in the rosary?" and "What are the origins of the rosary?" In chapter seven, we consider various ways to have more profound encounters with Jesus and Mary in this devotion—to enter into the prayers and mysteries we're to contemplate.

The last half of this book offers biblical reflections on the twenty mysteries of the rosary. Many people wonder, "What should I think about while meditating on the mysteries?" or, "How does this particular mystery relate to my life?" or "What are the practical implications for each of the mysteries?" These scriptural reflections will provide practical insights that help us not only *understand* the twenty mysteries but also *live* them.

GROUP STUDY QUESTIONS

1. Why are you reading this book about the rosary? What do you hope to receive from these pages?

2. What are some of the biggest challenges people have in praying the rosary?

3. How easy is it to pray the rosary in the midst of your busy life? What are some of the ways you can bring this devotion—even just part of it—into your daily life?

4. What new insight from this chapter did you find most helpful? How does it encourage you to incorporate the rosary a little more in your life?

CHAPTER TWO

The Wandering Mind
and Other Struggles

Do you ever wish you could pray the rosary better?

At first glance, the rosary should be a piece of cake for us Catholics. After all, it involves reciting a bunch of Our Fathers, Hail Marys, and Glory Bes—the ABC's of Catholic piety. You can't get much simpler than that, right? But if we're honest, most of us would probably admit that we've had our fair share of difficulties in praying this prayer.

For example, does your mind ever wander during the rosary? Despite our best intentions, we find ourselves thinking about anything except the mystery we're supposed to be contemplating. Instead of the annunciation, we're pondering what we're going to eat for dinner, some problem at work, what we're going to wear, or something someone said to us earlier in the day ("What did she *mean* by that?"). Suddenly we notice our mind is adrift, and we say to ourselves, "Wait, I'm supposed to be thinking about the angel Gabriel appearing to Mary!" At the end of the rosary, we feel as if we just rattled off a bunch of prayers while our hearts remained far removed from the mysteries of Christ.

At other times, we treat the rosary—much to our embarrassment—like a spiritual chore. It's something we know we should do, but we don't look forward to it. We pull out those beads to get a rosary in, but our hearts are not into the prayers. Maybe we show up at a Catholic event and see people handling the beads, and our hearts sink. We say to ourselves, "Oh, no. Not a *whole* rosary now! Maybe they'll just do a decade."

We might feel bad that we're not more enthusiastic. At the same time, we find ourselves anxious for the task to be completed. "We're only on the *second* sorrowful mystery?" Every decade feels like ten years! Again, we wish we had more fervor, but sometimes this is the reality we bring to our rosary praying.

Still another common scenario is after a long, tiring day, when we finally have a chance to sit down and rest in prayer with God. We pull out our beads, hoping to connect with Our Lord in this beautiful devotion. But what happens? Our head starts nodding, and we're falling asleep in the middle of a Hail Mary.

This is many people's real experience in praying the rosary. So if you have ever felt this way, know that you are in good company. Thousands of devout Catholics—young and old, men and women, lay people, priests, and religious—have told me how they love the rosary but struggle from time to time in praying it. I've had numerous bishops, men with the great gift of apostolic succession, tell me that they don't pray the rosary as well as they'd like! As one bishop in the Midwest told me many years ago, "Oh, the rosary! It's hard. I struggle all the time!"

Even the esteemed Cardinal Ratzinger, later Pope Benedict XVI, admitted that praying a whole rosary is often too much for him to do in a single sitting:

> I am too much of a restless spirit; I would wander too much. I take just one [set of mysteries], and then often only two or three mysteries out of the five, because I can then fit in a certain interval when I want to get away from work and free myself a bit, when I want to be quiet and to clear my head. A whole one would actually be too much for me then.[1]

Here's one crucial thing to keep in mind: Whatever struggles you may face with the rosary, never walk away feeling discouraged. If your mind wanders, if you don't feel the fervor, or if you're very sleepy while praying, remember that the words you are reciting are biblical and holy. Simply pulling out your beads and saying the sacred words is giving something beautiful to God, even if your heart or mind is not as into it as you'd like.

Moreover, as St. Thomas Aquinas taught, the intention to pray is itself the beginning of prayer. In fact, he wrote in his *Summa Theologiae*, "It is not necessary that prayer should be attentive throughout; because the force of the original intention with which one sets about praying renders the whole prayer meritorious."[2] If we sincerely desire to give God our best in the rosary, but we lose attention and fervor, that foundational good intention is still a beautiful gift to God. So even if our performance of the rosary is not as great as we'd like it to be, that doesn't wipe out the foundation of a good intention.

"Whatever struggles you may face with the rosary, never walk away feeling discouraged."

Writing Straight with Our Crooked Lines

I remember when my first child started drawing pictures, around the age of two. I'd come home from work, and she'd be eager to show me the pictures she had drawn for me during the day. Many times, the pictures were just a bunch of scribbles, not clear depictions one could easily identify. ("That's me? Oh…wow, I didn't realize… Well, thank you!") I was always delighted that my daughter was thinking of me during the day and desiring to give me a gift. I saw her heart more than her final product.

What would you think of a father who took his daughter's scribbled pictures, tore them up, and told her not to draw pictures again until she could get them exactly right? No good father would do that!

God looks at us the way a good dad looks at his son or daughter. When it comes to prayer, our heavenly Father sees our hearts, our sincere desires to pray well, not just our final products in prayer. So even if our praying of the rosary ends up being just a bunch of scribbles, we should remember that God can write straight with our crooked lines. He can delight in our good intentions, our sincere desires to please him in prayer, even if we lose fervor or our minds go someplace else. Having a good intention is more important than maintaining perfect *attention* throughout the prayer.

> "Who is it that wants us to think we're not good at this prayer? The enemy, the devil."

This, of course, is not an excuse to be lazy or careless in our praying. We must always strive to give our best. Trying to squeeze in a decade in between downs during your favorite team's game, for example, is probably not a sign of a good intention. Neither is checking your device for messages and alerts in between each decade. We must have a good intention. But if we get that right—if we come with a sincere desire to give God our best—then, even if we end up distracted, we must not lose heart and think our prayer is worthless.

Who is it that wants us to be discouraged about our rosary praying? Who is it that wants us to think we're not good at praying this prayer, that it's a waste of time, that it's pointless since we are so bad at it, that there are many other things we should be doing? The enemy, the devil, wants us to think that. He hates this prayer. And he will do everything he can to keep us from praying it, using even our humble and honest recognition that we're not reciting it as well as we should. He'll discourage us, getting us to think we're not worthy of this beautiful prayer.

Getting Better

At the same time, we should strive to get better at praying the rosary. If my daughter were sixteen years old and still couldn't draw a square, that would be a problem. Children need to develop their drawing abilities as they grow, and similarly, we children of God need to mature in our rosary praying throughout our lives, so that we can encounter Jesus more profoundly in this devotion. And that's what this book is all about.

So whether we're a beginners with a lot of questions about the rosary or avid devotees who have been reciting it for many years, we should all strive to meet Jesus and Mary more in this great devotion and experience the profound fruit the rosary can bear in our lives.

Let's turn our attention now to a common question people have about Mary and the rosary: Does the rosary give too much attention to Mary and not enough to God?

Group Study Questions

1. What is your biggest struggle in praying the rosary? How might you address that struggle?

2. Do you sometimes get discouraged over your struggles in prayer? What insights from this chapter offer you encouragement?

3. What setting (for example, before the Eucharist or outdoors, alone or with others) do you find most conducive to your prayer of the rosary?

4. St. Thérèse of Lisieux struggled with distractions in prayer, even falling asleep in the chapel! "Well, I am not desolate," she wrote. "I remember that little children are as pleasing to their parents when they are asleep as well as when they are wide awake; I remember, too, that when they perform operations, doctors put their patients to sleep. Finally, I remember that: 'The Lord knows our weakness, that he is mindful that we are but dust and ashes.'" How can our human weaknesses aid our prayer rather than detract from it?

CHAPTER THREE

Too Much Attention to Mary?

W hy do Catholics give so much attention to Mary?"

This is a question I have heard many times—from my Protestant friends and even a few Catholics. For some people, Catholic devotion to Mary can be scandalous. They might say, "Christians are called to worship Jesus Christ. Why do so many Catholic practices distract us from a personal relationship with Jesus by focusing so much on Mary?" While Mary may be a fine woman, a holy role model, and blessed to have served as the mother of the Messiah, she is not God. So why do Catholics treat her as if she were on par with God himself?

I can appreciate these concerns. After all, Catholicism does highlight Mary's role in God's plan of salvation more than any other religion. What other faith has so many statues, paintings, icons, and stained glass windows depicting Mary? What other religion proclaims as many doctrines that specifically involve the mother of Jesus—such as the Immaculate Conception, Mary's perpetual virginity, and her assumption into heaven? What other faith has so many songs dedicated to Mary (such as "Immaculate Mary" and "Hail, Holy Queen") and so many prayers addressed to her (such as the Hail Mary, the *Memorare*, and the Angelus)?

Then, of course, there is the rosary. This devotion stands out as one of the most perplexing of all Catholic practices involving Mary. In this prayer, Catholics recite five sets of ten Hail Marys. Each set, called a "decade," is introduced by the Our Father and concluded with praise of the Holy Trinity in a prayer known as the Glory Be. From an outsider's perspective, at the end of each decade of the rosary, the score seems to be:

God the Father: 1

The Holy Trinity: 1

Mary: 10

At best, all this repetitive attention given to Mary seems to be unbalanced and distracting from a relationship with Christ. At worst, this prayer seems to be a form of idolatry, treating Mary as if she were more important than God himself.

Before discussing the rosary itself, I want to address this uneasiness that some people feel about it. In this chapter, we will consider a few common questions about Mary and the rosary. It is my hope that addressing these questions will help us better appreciate the beauty of Marian devotion in our own lives and explain it more effectively to others.

"Why Do Catholics Worship Mary?"

In short, Catholics do not worship Mary.

To answer this question more fully, we must distinguish between "honor" and "worship." To honor someone is to show the person respect, recognizing a particular quality or excellence the person has achieved in life. Worship, on the other hand, denotes the homage and praise we give to God alone for who he is as the divine being.

Christians honor people all the time. We honor students for good grades by placing them on the dean's list. We honor employees by giving them pay raises. We honor athletes by presenting them with trophies, gold medals, and Super Bowl rings. When we as Christians honor people, we recognize the great things God has accomplished in their lives.

For example, as a professor, I *honor* my students when they graduate from college. I may applaud them at their commencement and congratulate them for completing their degrees. But I do not fall down on my knees and *worship* them as they walk out of the graduation ceremony! At the same time, the honor I give them does not in any manner take away from the worship I give to God. In fact, it enhances that worship, because in honoring my students, I am praising the one true God for giving them the talents and graces they needed to complete their program.

Similarly, Catholics *honor* Mary and the saints, but they do not *worship* them. And honoring Mary in no way distracts from our worship of God but actually enables us to praise God all the more.

If someone wants to praise an artist, he does so by admiring his art. Leonardo da Vinci would not be upset with people who admire the gaze of his *Mona Lisa*, and Michelangelo would not be angry with people who admire his "Last Judgment" scene in the Sistine Chapel. No artist would rush into a museum and say, "Stop looking at my works of art! Stop talking about my paintings! You should give all your attention to *me*!" Rather, the artist is praised when his masterpieces are recognized and celebrated.

In a similar way, God is a divine artist, and his spiritual masterpieces are the saints. The saints are men and women who have been completely transformed by God's saving grace. We give God great praise when we thank him for the work of salvation he has accomplished in their lives.

Furthermore, taking time to recognize God's works in this world is very biblical. The scriptural writers, in fact, were very comfortable with admiring the beauty of God's creation. Psalm 104, for example, praises God for the sun, the moon, the mountains, and the seas. Such recognition does not get in the way of our worshiping God but rather allows us to praise him even more by thanking him for the splendor of his creation.

If the Bible encourages us to praise God for his *natural* works of creation, how much more should we praise him for his *supernatural* works—for taking weak, fragile human beings and transforming them by his grace into holy sons and daughters of God! When Catholics honor the saints, it is as if we are saying, "Praise be to you, Jesus, for what you did in the life of St. Paul!" or, "Thank you, Lord, for giving us St. Francis of Assisi as a model of holiness."

Not only is it OK to honor Mary and the rest of the saints, but we actually give God more praise when we recognize his redemptive work perfected in them.

> "Not only is it OK to honor Mary and the saints, but we actually give God more praise."

"Why Do Catholics Pray to Mary?"

Rather than say Catholics pray to Mary, it may be better to say that we ask her to pray for us. Yet some people may wonder, "Why not go to God directly?" After all, St. Paul taught that "there is one mediator between God and men, the man Jesus Christ" (1 Timothy 2:5). Why do Catholics place Mary as an extra layer of mediation between men and God?

First, Christ's role as the "one mediator between God and men" in no way excludes the notion of Christians praying for one another.[1] In fact, Paul instructs Christians to intercede for one another (see 1 Timothy 2:1). He even commands that people pray for him and his ministry: "You also must help us by prayer, so that many will give thanks on our behalf for the blessing granted us in answer to many prayers" (2 Corinthians 1:11). Paul's asking other Christians to pray for him seems quite natural. No one would accuse him of not going directly to God with his needs.

Clearly, the importance of Christians praying for each other is rooted in Scripture. And once we understand the profound communion existing between the saints in heaven and Christians here on earth, then the notion of Mary and the saints interceding for us will make a lot of sense.

The saints are our brothers and sisters in Christ who have gone before us. They have faced many of the struggles and trials we endure as Christians, and they have made it to the other side. Though they have died and gone to heaven, they continue to be united to us through our common bond in Christ. From

> "God does not get jealous when we ask others to pray for us."

a biblical perspective, they are not dead but spiritually alive in the arms of God (see Luke 20:38) and, in a sense, closer to us now than when they were on the earth. Indeed, the Letter to the Hebrews portrays the assembly of the saints in heaven not as a congregation far removed from the events of this world but as a "great cloud of witnesses" that surrounds us in the drama of our daily lives (see Hebrews 12:1). As our older brothers and sisters in Christ, they continue to pray for us, that we may persevere in the faith and one day join them in heaven (see Revelation 5:8; 8:3).

Whether it be among Christians here on earth or with the saints in heaven, intercession is a way that we show our love for God and build up the body of Christ. When someone asked Jesus what were the greatest of the commandments, he responded: "You shall love the Lord your God with all your heart...[and] love your neighbor as yourself" (Matthew 22:37, 39). The Christian life can be summed up in these two themes, love of God and love of neighbor. In fact, we show our love for God by loving our neighbor. And one of the best ways we can grow in fellowship with our neighbor is through prayer: praying for others and sharing our needs with them so they might pray for us.

This is why seeking the intercession of Mary and the saints in no way distracts us from our relationship with God but rather deepens our unity in God's family. God does not get jealous when we ask others to pray for us. For example, as a father, I am delighted when I see my children getting along so well that they turn to each other with their needs. Imagine if my toddler son were to ask his older sister to help him count or help him say his prayers, and I were to get angry with him, saying, "Son, I feel so left out! Why are you asking your sister for help? Why don't you come to me directly with your needs?"

Such an attitude would be strange indeed! As a father, I do not view my children's love for each other as competition for love and attention that should be given to me. Rather, I rejoice all the more when I see my children asking each other for help and lovingly responding to each other's needs. In a similar way, our heavenly Father rejoices when he sees his sons and daughters loving each other so much that they ask each other for prayer and intercede for each other's needs.

That is why the real question is not, "Is it OK to ask Mary and the saints to pray for us?" but rather, "Do you want to love God with all your heart?" We love God by loving all our brothers and sisters, including Mary and the saints, and we deepen our Christian fellowship by praying for one another and asking each other for prayer. In fact, the *Catechism of the Catholic Church* teaches that living in communion with the saints leads us closer to Jesus:

> Exactly as Christian communion among our fellow pilgrims brings us closer to Christ, so our communion with the saints joins us to Christ, from whom as from its fountain and head issues all grace, and the life of the People of God itself. (*CCC*, 957)

GROUP STUDY QUESTIONS

1. Mary is "blessed…among women," and "all generations will call [her] blessed" (Luke 1:42, 48). How do you honor Mary? If you hesitate to do so, what light has this chapter shed on your questions about Marian devotion?

2. In what ways does honoring Mary glorify God?

3. How aware are you of the "cloud of witnesses" that surrounds you?

4. Who is your favorite saint? How does he or she help deepen your union with God?

5. Pope St. John Paul II speaks of a "school of Mary," which is the practice of "contemplating the scenes of the Rosary in union with Mary" (*RVM*, 14). Why is Mary a good teacher of the Gospel?

CHAPTER FOUR

The Hail Mary:
Jesus at the Center

At first glance, the Hail Mary seems to be primarily about Mary. However, as St. John Paul II emphasized, this prayer is meant to focus our attention on Jesus Christ. "Although the repeated Hail Mary is addressed directly to Mary, it is to Jesus that the act of love is ultimately directed" (*RVM*, 26).

We can see this in the first part of this prayer, which is drawn from the words that the angel Gabriel and Elizabeth used to greet the mother of the Messiah. These words do not focus primarily on Mary but on what John Paul II calls "the wonder of heaven and earth" over the mystery of the Incarnation taking place inside her.

First, imagine being the archangel Gabriel. You've existed long before the Blessed Virgin Mary was born, before the village of Nazareth was built, before the people of Israel were established. Indeed, you've existed before the sun, moon, stars, and planet Earth were created. And from before the creation of the world, you have been worshiping and adoring the all-mighty, all-powerful, infinite God.

But one day, this all-holy God sends you down to this little planet called Earth, to visit an obscure village called Nazareth and talk to a tiny creature, a woman named Mary, and announce to her that the all-powerful, all-holy, infinite God you've been adoring since before creation is about to enter time and space and become a little baby in her womb! In awe over the mystery of God becoming man inside Mary, Gabriel says, "Hail, full of grace, the Lord is with you" (Luke 1:28).

Indeed, the Lord is with Mary as he has never been with anyone else from the beginning of time!

Similarly, consider Elizabeth's words to Mary. Elizabeth, the Bible tells us, is "filled with the Holy Spirit" (Luke 2:41). That means she has been given prophetic insight. So she knows that Mary is pregnant not with any ordinary child but with the holy Son of God. And in wonder over that mystery of Mary's son, Elizabeth exclaims, "Blessed are you among women!... for blessed is the fruit of your womb" (Luke 2: 42).

This is what the Hail Mary is all about. Every time we say the Hail Mary, we enter into that ecstatic praise of heaven and earth over the mystery of Christ—*heaven* represented by Gabriel, and *earth* represented by Elizabeth. By repeating these biblical words in the Hail Mary, we participate in heaven and earth's joyful response to the mystery of God becoming man. As Pope John Paul II explains,

> These words...could be said to give a glimpse of God's own wonderment as he contemplates his "masterpiece"—the Incarnation of the Son in the womb of the Virgin Mary.... The repetition of the Hail Mary in the Rosary gives us a share in God's own wonder and pleasure: in jubilant amazement we acknowledge the greatest miracle of history. (*RVM*, 33)

"Pray for Us..."

In the second part of the Hail Mary, we entrust our lives to Mary's intercession: "Holy Mary, mother of God, pray for us sinners, now and at the hour of our death. Amen." Even this part of the Hail Mary is meant to lead us to Christ. We ask Mary to pray for us to be faithful in our walk with the Lord, now and up to the moment of our death.

As a model disciple of Christ, Mary consented to God's will when the angel Gabriel appeared to her (see Luke 1:38), and she persevered in faith throughout her life (see John 19:25–27; Acts 1:14). Consequently, she is the ideal person to be praying for us, praying that we may walk in faith as she did. The *Catechism of the Catholic Church* explains, "She prays for us as she prayed for herself: 'Let it be to me according to your word.' By entrusting ourselves to her prayer, we abandon ourselves to the will of God together with her: 'Thy will be done'" (*CCC*, 2677).

JESUS: THE CENTER OF GRAVITY

After these opening lines, we come to the climax of the Hail Mary: "And blessed is the fruit of thy womb, Jesus." John Paul II says that Jesus's holy name not only serves as the hinge joining the two parts of the Hail Mary but also is this prayer's very "center of gravity" (*RVM*, 33). Indeed, the Hail Mary is meant to lead us to the person of Jesus, and at the center of this prayer, we speak his sacred name.

> "Every time we say the Hail Mary, we enter into that ecstatic praise of heaven and earth over the mystery of Christ."

But sometimes when we pray the rosary too quickly we miss this important moment.

> Sometimes, in a hurried recitation, this center of gravity can be overlooked, and with it the connection to the mystery of Christ being contemplated. Yet it is precisely the emphasis given to the name of Jesus and to his mystery that is the sign of a meaningful and fruitful recitation of the Rosary. (*RVM*, 33)

I once attended what may have been the fastest rosary on earth. A group of people at a parish in the Midwest prayed the rosary every day before Mass. It was a nine-minute rosary. They sounded like auctioneers! God bless them for praying the rosary daily, when many people had jettisoned this prayer. But I think John Paul II would invite them, and all of us, to make sure we take time to give due reverence to the holy name of Jesus each time it is spoken.

A friend of mine suggests that we treat the name of Jesus in the Hail Mary like a speed bump: Slow down as you approach it, and speak it with care and attention. "Blessed is the fruit of thy womb,... *Jesus*." Let's speak Jesus's name with tender love at every Hail Mary in the rosary. Indeed, we should never neglect the power of Christ's name—the only name under heaven by which we may hope in salvation (see Acts 4:12).

From a biblical perspective, the very fact that we can call upon the name of Jesus is astonishing. In the Old Testament, the Jews approached God's name with such reverence that eventually their tradition avoided saying it. They often called on God in prayer using the title "Lord." However, since God has entered into humanity in Christ, we now have the privilege of calling on the personal name of the Lord, Jesus (*CCC*, 2666).

> "Let's speak Jesus's name with tender love at every Hail Mary in the Rosary."

Christians throughout the centuries have found in the name of Jesus a source of strength and meditation. The Hail Mary leads us to that divine source, as we utter the sacred name at its center.

Group Study Questions

1. Pope St. John Paul II called the rosary "at heart a Christocentric prayer" (*RVM*, 1). How is Christ at the center of the rosary? Why is this important?

2. Why is Mary a good intercessor for us?

3. This chapter explained how in every Hail Mary we enter the praise of Gabriel and Elizabeth over the mystery of Christ. How might this insight change the way you pray the Hail Mary?

4. Say the Hail Mary slowly. What new insight does this give you?

5. What challenges did Mary face? How did her *fiat*, "Let it be to me according to your word," empower her life?

CHAPTER FIVE

Repetition:
You Can Never Say "I Love You" Enough

Why do Catholics repeat so many prayers? Don't they know that Jesus condemned vain repetition? In the Sermon on the Mount, Jesus said, "And in praying do not heap up empty phrases as the Gentiles do; for they think that they will be heard for their many words. Do not be like them, for your Father knows what you need before you ask him" (Matthew 6:7–8).

For some people, the rosary appears to be the kind of repetitious prayer Jesus was condemning. With Hail Mary after Hail Mary, the rosary may seem to be a dry, mechanical way of praying to God. "We should talk to God as a personal friend would, not as a robot." It is thus alleged that the rosary is vain repetition, not true, intimate prayer flowing from the heart. Shouldn't Christians speak more openly to Jesus, rather than relying on formulas repeated over and over again?

In response, first we must point out that Jesus does not condemn *all* types of repetition in prayer. Rather, he is criticizing the gentile practice of reciting endless formulas and divine names, hoping to say the words that would force the gods to answer their petitions. Jesus condemns this pagan approach of trying to get God to answer prayer through magical formulas. He challenges us to approach our heavenly Father not as the pagans do their deities but rather in confident trust, knowing that "your Father knows what you need before you ask him" (Matthew 6:8). Indeed, he knows what we need better than we do, and he provides for those needs even before we realize them (see Matthew 6:25–34).

Moreover, we know Jesus cannot be condemning all forms of repetition because, in the very next verse, he gives us a formula prayer to recite: the Our Father. Jesus says, "Pray then like this: Our Father, who art in heaven, hallowed be thy name..." (Matthew 6:9–13). Furthermore, Jesus himself repeats his prayers. In the Garden of Gethsemane, Jesus speaks the same prayer three times: "Leaving them again, he went away and prayed for the third time, saying the same words" (Matthew 26:44). No one would accuse Jesus of vain repetition!

Similarly, in the Old Testament, parts of Psalm 118 are structured around the repeated phrase "His steadfast love endures forever," and the book of Daniel presents the three men in the fiery furnace constantly repeating, "Sing praise to him and highly exalt him forever" (see Daniel 3:52–68). God does not condemn these ancient Jews for vain repetition but rather looks favorably on their prayers and answers them (see Psalm 118:21).

> "Repetition is part of the language of love."

In the New Testament, the book of Revelation describes how the four living creatures repeat the same prayer of praise for all eternity. Gathered around God's throne, "day and night they never cease to sing, 'Holy, holy, holy, is the Lord God Almighty, who was and is and is to come!'" (Revelation 4:8). Thus, the worship of God in heaven involves words of holy praise that are repeated without end.

In sum, although the pagan approach of trying to manipulate God by vain repetition is always wrong, proper repetitious prayer is very biblical and pleasing to God. But we may still wonder *why* there is so much repetition in the rosary.

Prayer with a Purpose

The purpose of repeating prayers is not repetition for its own sake. Rather, the peaceful rhythm created by reciting familiar words from Scripture is meant to slow down our minds and spirits so that we can prayerfully reflect on different aspects of Christ's life.

As I mentioned earlier, the pope notes in his letter that this devotion is similar to the "Jesus Prayer" that people have recited for centuries. Christians slowly repeat the words "Jesus Christ, Son of God, have mercy on me, a sinner" often following the rhythm of their breathing. The lingering pace of this prayer whispered over and over again is meant to calm the mind so that we may be disposed to meet God in prayer.

The succession of Hail Marys in the rosary is meant to achieve the same purpose. It helps us follow the exhortation of Psalm 46:10: "Be still, and know that I am God." One Catholic theologian explains it like this:

> Masters in the Buddhist tradition of meditation speak of "calming the monkey mind." This means the settling of the superficial mind which dances and darts from preoccupation to preoccupation and whose concerns tend to dominate our consciousness: "What is my next appointment? Where do I go next? What did she mean by that?" In order to open up the deepest ground of the soul,… the mind must be, at least for a time, quelled. In the rosary meditation, the mantra of the repeated Hail Marys quiets the monkey mind, compelling it to cede place to deeper reaches of the psyche.[1]

THE HEARTBEAT OF THE ROSARY

On another level, the pope encourages us to view the repetition of Hail Marys not as a superficial, mechanical exercise, which indeed would be rather boring and empty of life, but rather as an expression proper to a relationship of love. For example, I may tell my wife several times a day, "I love you." I may say these words to her as I go out the door for work in the morning or just before we fall asleep at night. On special occasions, I may write these words in a card. When we are out for dinner on a date, I may look her in the eyes and say, "I love you."

Although my wife has heard me say these same words to her thousands of times, never once has she complained, "Stop saying the same thing over and over again! I can't take all this vain repetition!" In an intimate, personal relationship such as marriage, two people may repeat to each other certain expressions of love, and each time the words express the heartfelt affection they have for one another. Indeed, repetition is part of the language of love.

This is the proper context for understanding the repeated prayers in the rosary. We have an intimate, personal relationship with Jesus Christ. In reciting the Hail Mary throughout the rosary, we participate over and over again in the wonder-filled response of Gabriel and Elizabeth to the mystery of Christ. Bead after bead, we ask Mary to pray for us, that we may be drawn closer to her son. And most of all, prayer after prayer, *we affectionately repeat the name of our Beloved* in the very center of each Hail Mary: "Blessed is the fruit of thy womb, *Jesus.*"

> "The name of Jesus, spoken with tender love, becomes the heartbeat of the rosary."

Indeed, the name of Jesus, spoken with tender love, becomes the heartbeat of the rosary. John Paul II says the rosary should be thought of as "an outpouring of that love which tirelessly returns to the person loved with expressions similar in their content but ever fresh in terms of the feeling pervading them.... To understand the Rosary, one has to enter into the psychological dynamic proper to love" (*RVM*, 26).

GROUP STUDY QUESTIONS

1. "To understand the Rosary, one has to enter into the psychological dynamic proper to love" (*RVM*, 26). What is this dynamic? How do human relationships of love shed light on the repetition in the rosary?
2. How does the pagan "vain repetition" differ from the vocal prayer of the Church?

3. What words do you use to convey love to others? To God?

4. How can the repetition in the rosary deepen your intimacy with God?

CHAPTER SIX

The Origins of the Rosary

According to one tradition, the rosary's defining moment came during an apparition of Mary to St. Dominic around the year 1221. Dominic was combating a popular heresy in France called Albigensianism. Mary gave him the rosary, told him to teach people this devotion, and promised that his apostolic efforts would be blessed with much success if he did. We know the religious order Dominic founded (the Dominicans) clearly played a major role in promoting the rosary throughout the world in the early years of this devotion.

THE POOR MAN'S BREVIARY

Another important development in the history of the rosary is found in its roots in the liturgical prayer of the Church. In the medieval period, there was a desire to give the laity a form of common prayer similar to that of the monasteries. Monastic prayer was structured around the Psalter—the recitation of all 150 psalms from the Bible. At that time, however, most laity could not afford a Psalter, and most could not even read.

As a parallel to the monastic reading of the 150 psalms, the practice developed among the laity of praying the Our Father 150 times throughout the day. This devotion came to be known as "the poor man's breviary." The laity eventually were given beads to help them count their prayers.

Marian devotion followed a similar pattern. Gabriel's words, "Hail Mary, full of grace, the Lord is with you" (Luke 1:28), sometimes were read in the monasteries at the end of a psalm, showing how the psalms found fulfillment in the New Testament with the coming of Christ through the Virgin Mary. Some laity began to recite these words in the manner of the Our Father—150 times, while counting their prayers on beads. In repeating the words of Gabriel, they were reliving the joy of the annunciation and celebrating the mystery of God becoming man in Mary's womb.

Christians linked this prayer with Elizabeth's words to Mary at the Visitation: "Blessed are you among women, and blessed is the fruit of your womb" (Luke 1:42). Finally, with the addition of the name "Jesus" in the thirteenth century, the first half of the Hail Mary was in place.

> "This early form of the Hail Mary was recited 150 times on the beads."

This early form of the Hail Mary was recited 150 times on the beads. By the fifteenth century, the 150 Hail Marys had been divided into sets of ten, known as "decades," with an Our Father at the beginning of each.

Meditating on Mysteries

Another line of development in monastic prayer eventually led to the practice of contemplating Christ's life while reciting the Hail Marys. Some monasteries began associating the psalms with an aspect of Jesus's life. At the end of each psalm, the monks would recite a phrase relating that psalm to the life of Jesus or Mary. Taken together, these phrases formed a brief life of Christ and his mother.

A devotion that joined fifty of these phrases with the praying of fifty Hail Marys began in the early fifteenth century. However, since fifty points of reflection generally could not be recalled without a book, the devotion was simplified by reducing the meditation points to fifteen, with one for every decade. Thus, by the end of the fifteenth century, the basic structure of the rosary was in place: Our Fathers dividing decades of Hail Marys, with meditations on the life of Christ and Mary.

In the sixteenth century, the sets of five Joyful, five Sorrowful, and five Glorious Mysteries as we know them today began to emerge. Also, the vocal prayers of the rosary were finalized. The Glory Be was added to the end of every decade, and the second half of the Hail Mary was formalized: "Holy Mary, Mother of God, pray for us sinners now and at the hour of our death. Amen." In 1569, Pope St. Pius V officially approved the rosary in this form: fifteen decades of Hail Marys introduced by the Our Father and concluded with the Glory Be.

> "You know you are living in a historic moment when *USA Today* is teaching people how to pray the rosary."

And so the rosary remained for over four centuries. Then, in 2002, Pope St. John Paul II proposed something new.

THE LUMINOUS MYSTERIES

You know you are living in a historic moment when *USA Today* is teaching people how to pray the rosary. Its October 17, 2002, edition featured an article that included a typical *USA Today* visual aid graphic with very atypical content: a diagram of the rosary. The graphic offered clear instructions on how to pray the rosary, explaining which prayer— Our Father, Hail Mary, or Glory Be—should be recited with which bead. While one might expect to find such a picture and explanation in pamphlets in the back of a church, it was surprising to find it in the pages of the secular press and, no less, in one of our nation's most widely read newspapers.

What was the impulse for such catechetical instruction in this most unusual of settings?

The day before the article's publication, Pope John Paul II published his Apostolic Letter on the Most Holy Rosary, *Rosarium Virginis Mariae*. As mentioned in chapter one, the letter announced the Year of the Rosary and called on Catholics to renew their devotion to this traditional prayer. However, what grabbed the attention of *USA Today* and the entire Catholic world was John Paul II's proposal of a whole new set of mysteries for contemplation in the rosary, the "Mysteries of Light" or "Luminous Mysteries."

John Paul II suggested that reflection on the mysteries of Christ's public ministry would help Catholics enter more fully into the life of Jesus through the rosary: "To bring out fully the Christological depth of the Rosary it would be suitable to make an addition to the traditional pattern which...could broaden it to include the mysteries of Christ's public ministry between his Baptism and his passion" (*RVM*, 19). The pope proposed the following scenes to be contemplated: (1) Christ's baptism, (2) the wedding feast at Cana, (3) the proclamation of the kingdom, (4) the Transfiguration, and (5) the institution of the Eucharist.

The pope's invitation to reflect on these mysteries makes a lot of sense. As some have noted, in the traditional form of the rosary, the transition from the fifth Joyful Mystery to the first Sorrowful Mystery seemed rather abrupt. We moved from Jesus as a twelve-year-old boy found by his parents in the temple to Jesus as a thirty-three-year-old man about to be crucified on Calvary. The Mysteries of Light fill in the gap.

The pope also said he hoped the addition of new mysteries would give the rosary "fresh life" at a time when the rosary was devalued in many parts of the Church. He hoped this new vitality would help "enkindle renewed interest in the Rosary's place within Christian spirituality as a true doorway to the depths of the Heart of Christ, ocean of joy and of light, of suffering and of glory" (*RVM*, 19). Indeed, the Mysteries of Light seem to be not only a most fitting development of the rosary but also a providential one for our age and one that is likely to stand the test of time.

GROUP STUDY QUESTIONS

1. What insight about the history of the rosary did you find most interesting? Why?

2. Explain in your own words the connection between the rosary and the monastic practice of praying the 150 Psalms. How might the rosary's connection to the psalms inspire the way you'd like to pray the rosary?

3. The Vatican Council document *Lumen Gentium* begins, "Christ is the Light of nations. Because this is so, this Sacred Synod gathered together in the Holy Spirit eagerly desires, by proclaiming the Gospel to every creature, to bring the light of Christ to all men." How might the Luminous Mysteries help us respond to the council's call to proclaim the Gospel?

4. What were the circumstances of your first encounter with the rosary? Who introduced you to this devotion? How did you respond?

CHAPTER SEVEN

More than Words
Ten Ways to Encounter Jesus More in the Rosary

Pope Paul VI once said, "Without contemplation, the Rosary is a body without a soul, and its recitation runs the risk of becoming a mechanical repetition of formulas."[1] The body of the rosary is the prayers we recite with our lips (Our Father, Hail Mary, Glory Be), while its soul is our contemplation of the mysteries of Christ. Up to this point, we have discussed primarily the body of the rosary. Now let us consider its soul.

With each decade of the rosary, we are to reflect on a different aspect of Christ's life and work of salvation. As we move from one mystery to the next, it is as if we are looking at pictures from the life of Jesus Christ, from his childhood and ministry as an adult to his death and resurrection at the culmination of his messianic mission.[2]

This is why John Paul II said the rosary is truly a Christ-centered prayer. It is "a compendium" of the entire Gospel, because it presents us with images from God's plan of redemption as fulfilled in Jesus (*RVM*, 1). By continuously reflecting on the mysteries, we can participate today in those saving events made present to us. Thus, the rhythm of the rosary can begin to shape the daily rhythm of our lives.[3]

John Paul II offers several suggestions to help us enter more profoundly into the mysteries so that the rosary can serve as an even greater source of strength and guidance for our daily lives. Many of these are based on the way he himself prayed the rosary. Let us consider ten of those insights.

1. Announce Each Mystery and Visualize It

John Paul II recommends that, at the start of each decade, we pause to prepare our minds to reflect on that decade's particular mystery from Christ's life. This is an important first step, for our preparation can set the tone for the entire decade. It can help determine whether the following ten Hail Marys will be a dry, mechanical repetition of a formula or a pathway to union with Christ.

After announcing the mystery at the beginning of each decade, the pope encourages us to use our imaginations "to open up a scenario on which to focus our attention" (*RVM*, 29). One way of concentrating our attention may be to look at an icon or image from religious art that portrays the mystery.

"Without contemplation, the Rosary is a body without a soul."
—Paul VI

Another approach the pope suggests is the Ignatian method of prayer. St. Ignatius of Loyola recommended that Christians use their minds and imaginations to place themselves reflectively in the scene that is being contemplated.

For example, when praying the first Joyful Mystery, the annunciation, we might imagine what it would have been like to be in the Virgin Mary's home when the angel appeared to her in Nazareth. We can picture the young Mary, perhaps alone in a room praying or doing some work around the house. Suddenly an angel of the Lord appears to her. What does the angel look like? What is Mary's first reaction? What is the look on her face?

We listen to the angel assure Mary not to be afraid and then announce that she is to become the mother of Israel's Messiah. The Jews had been waiting hundreds of years for God to send them the Messiah and free them from their sufferings, and now Mary learns that she is the one who will give birth to this king. Even more astonishing is the fact that she will conceive this child not through natural means but as a virgin, by the power of God's Spirit!

A lot is being asked of this young woman from Nazareth. How will she respond? Is she afraid? We wait for her answer. Then we picture her, with total trust, saying to the Lord's messenger, "Let it be done unto me according to your word" (Luke 1:38). Now the God of the universe will become a baby in her womb.

This Ignatian method of visualizing biblical scenes also invites us to use our senses. We can imagine the sights, sounds, and smells of each scene as if we were there. Let us consider the second luminous mystery, the wedding at Cana, in this way.

Imagine being in a small Galilean village for a first-century Jewish wedding feast. We picture ourselves arriving at a joyful celebration. As we move through the crowd, we hear a lot of music, singing, laughter, and conversation. We smell the aroma coming from the many tables of food. We see the bride and groom smiling and laughing with their families. We also see Mary, Jesus, and some of his disciples enjoying the festivities.

Amid this great feast, we see Mary with a troubled look on her face as she speaks with a few of the servants. She then rushes over to Jesus. There is a mini-crisis, but no one else seems to notice. Mary informs Jesus that the party has run out of wine. What will Jesus do? What *can* he do? Will he send his disciples to get more wine? Will he make wine appear out of nowhere? Mary tells the servants to do whatever her son tells them.

Surprisingly, Jesus simply commands the servants to fill the ritual purification jars with water and serve it to the people. "How will this solve the problem?" we wonder. The servants perhaps think this is some practical joke: Have the people drunk so much wine that they won't even notice that water is now being served?

We stay to watch how this wine will go over with the steward of the feast. He takes a drink from the jars, and we are shocked to see him smile at the taste of it and hear him praise the bridegroom for serving such great wine: "Every man serves the good wine first; and when men have drunk freely, then the poor wine; but you have kept the good wine until now" (John 2:10).

We now taste the wine for ourselves, and sure enough, it is the best wine we have ever had. We realize what has happened: The water was changed into wine. Jesus has just performed the first of his miracles here at the wedding feast in Cana.

Applying our imagination and our senses to the biblical scenes of Christ's life is an approach that flows from the mystery of the Incarnation itself. As John Paul II explains, by becoming a man and dwelling among us, God chose to reveal himself to us in a way that appeals to the senses. "In Jesus, God wanted to take on human features. It is through his bodily reality that we are led into contact with the mystery of his divinity" (*RVM*, 29).

2. Listening to the Word of God

Another way to prepare for our reflection on the mysteries is to read from Sacred Scripture at the beginning of each decade. Depending on the circumstances, such a reading could be long (for example, reading the entire account of the annunciation) or short (reading only a few lines from the scene). This is not simply a matter of recalling more information for our meditation but of allowing God to speak to our hearts in a unique way.

Scripture is the inspired Word of God; contact with this sacred Word can be life-transforming. The Letter to the Hebrews says, "The word of God is living and active, sharper than any two-edged sword, piercing to the division of soul and spirit, of joints and marrow, and discerning the thoughts and intentions of the heart" (Hebrews 4:12).

The pope encourages us to encounter the living Christ while listening to the inspired Word of God during the rosary: "No other words can ever match the efficacy of the inspired word. As we listen, we are certain that this is the word of God, spoken for today and spoken 'for me'" (*RVM*, 30).

In harmony with this approach, chapters 8 through 11 of this book offer biblical reflections on the twenty mysteries. These reflections uncover the historical context, Old Testament background, and spiritual significance of each biblical scene related to the mysteries of Christ in the rosary. And chapter 12 offers a "Scriptural Rosary"—a list of ten verses one can read or reflect on while praying the ten Hail Marys for each decade. It is my hope that these verses will draw readers more deeply into God's Word and enrich their contemplation of these mysteries of salvation.

3. Silence

Next, John Paul II suggests that we pause in silence and take time to ponder the mystery before beginning the vocal prayers of the rosary, the Our Father, Hail Mary, and Glory Be. This gives us the opportunity at the start of each decade to reflect on the words from Scripture and allow them to soak into our souls.

In a society dominated by technology and mass media, interior silence can be difficult to find. Images from various screens race across our minds and compete for our attention, while sounds from our devices or our favorite songs constantly fill our heads. Our society is afraid of silence. Yet it is in silence that God speaks to our hearts (see *CCC*, 2717). John Paul II challenges us to rest in that silence, even briefly, at the start of each decade so that we might be more open to God's speaking to our hearts in the rosary.

One helpful method for entering into that silence is to focus on one word from the biblical account representing the mystery. Another is to picture just one image from the mystery being contemplated. If given attention, this moment of silence can help settle the soul, calm our scattered thoughts, and direct our attention to God in preparation for the next ten beads.

4. The Our Father: Praying in Union with God's Family

After focusing on the mystery, we begin our vocal prayers by lifting our minds to God the Father. In reciting the Our Father, we express two amazing truths about the Christian life.

First, because of our union with Christ, we truly can call God "Abba"—a term of intimate affection that Jewish children used to address their dads (see Romans 8:15; Galatians 4:6; *RVM*, 32). Despite our weaknesses and repeated failings, God has forgiven our sins, and we can approach him with confidence. We can call him "Abba." By starting each decade of the rosary with this prayer, we begin our reflection on the life of the Son in union with the gaze from his Father in heaven.

Secondly, the Our Father expresses our unity with all other Christians. Jesus does not tell us to call God simply "*My* Father" but "*Our* Father." This subtle first word of the Lord's Prayer reminds us that Christianity is not a religion of our own isolated, private relationship with God. Jesus did not come to save us as islands separate from one another. In reconciling us to God, Christ reconciles us to each other. He unites us as brothers and sisters under one heavenly Father, *our* Father. Therefore, the Our Father is truly a prayer of the whole family of God, expressing our unity with all our brothers and sisters in Christ throughout the world and throughout time.

John Paul II highlights the profound communal nature of this prayer in the rosary. He explains that the Our Father recited at the start of each decade "makes meditation upon the mystery, even when carried out in solitude, an ecclesial experience"—an experience of the whole Church (*RVM*, 32). In this sense, we can say that we never pray the rosary in isolation. Whether we are praying it at home, in a car, on a business trip, in the hospital, or in a nursing home, the Our Fathers underscore the fact that we pray in union with our friends, our family, our fellow Christians here on earth, and even the saints in heaven.

> "It is as if we are gathered in our Father's arms to look at 'pictures' from the life of our eldest brother, Jesus."

When we pray the rosary, it is as if we are gathered in our Father's arms with all our brothers and sisters throughout the ages to look at pictures from the life of our eldest brother, Jesus. In this spiritual family album, we remember and celebrate the key moments of Christ's life—such as the announcement of his birth in Nazareth, his being born in Bethlehem, his ministry in Galilee, his death and resurrection in Jerusalem, and his ascension into heaven. Over and over again, these images of salvation pass before the eyes of our souls as we pray and ponder with his mother, Mary.

5. The Ten Hail Marys: Contemplating Christ with His Mother

In chapter 4, we considered how the Hail Mary truly is a Christ-centered prayer. In the first part of this prayer, we repeat Gabriel's and Elizabeth's joyful responses to the mystery of God becoming man in Mary's womb: "Hail Mary, full of grace, the Lord is with thee. Blessed art thou among women, and blessed is the fruit of your womb." Thus, in each Hail Mary, we have the opportunity to participate in this awe-filled wonder over Jesus while reflecting on the mysteries of salvation.

The pope offers one suggestion on how we can give special attention to Christ's name in the rosary. After saying "Jesus" in each Hail Mary, we can add a clause related to the mystery being contemplated. For example, in the first sorrowful mystery (the agony in the garden), we could say, "...and blessed is the fruit of thy womb, Jesus, *agonizing in the garden*." In the fifth glorious mystery (the crowning of Mary), we could pray, "...and blessed is the fruit of thy womb, Jesus, *who crowned you as Queen of Heaven and Earth*."

John Paul II says this popular practice, which was spread by St. Louis de Montfort and others, "gives forceful expression to our faith in Christ, directed to the different moments of the Redeemer's life. It is at once *a profession of faith* and an aid in concentrating our meditation" (*RVM*, 33).

In the last part of the Hail Mary, we ask Mary to intercede for us as we ponder the mysteries of Christ. John Paul II explains that contemplation is simply looking upon the face of Jesus. Since no one has devoted himself to this loving task more than Christ's mother, it makes sense that Christians would want to gaze upon the face of Jesus in union with her.

In a unique way, the face of the Son belongs to Mary. It was in her womb that Christ was formed, receiving from her a human resemblance, which points to an even greater spiritual closeness. The eyes of her heart already turned to him at the annunciation, when she conceived him by the power of the Holy Spirit. In the months that followed, she began to sense his presence and to picture his features. When at last she gave birth to him in Bethlehem, her eyes were able to gaze tenderly on the face of her Son, as she "wrapped him in swaddling cloths, and laid him in a manger" (Luke 2:7). Thereafter Mary's gaze, ever filled with adoration and wonder, would never leave him. (*RVM*, 10)

John Paul II goes on to note that Mary was with Jesus at his first miracle at Cana, where she anticipated his desire to change the water into wine (see John 2:4). She watched her son die on the cross, but her sorrow turned to radiant joy when he rose from the dead. As the pope explains, "No one knows Christ better than Mary; no one can introduce us to a profound knowledge of his mystery better than his Mother" (*RVM*, 14). No one has contemplated his life more than Mary.

This is why it is fitting to ask for Our Lady's intercession as we reflect on Christ's birth, life, death, and resurrection in the rosary. "Contemplating the scenes of the Rosary in union with Mary is a means of learning from her to 'read' Christ, to discover his secrets and to understand his message" (*RVM*, 14). Mary can draw us more deeply into Christ through her loving prayers for us—both "now" as we pray the rosary and "at the hour of our death."

6. The Glory Be: The Height of Our Contemplation

Glory be to the Father, and to the Son, and to the Holy Spirit, as it was in the beginning, is now and ever shall be, world without end. Amen.

This short prayer of praise known as the Glory Be comes at the end of each decade, but it is not simply a closing prayer. Rather it is meant to express the peak of our contemplation.

Praise of the Holy Trinity is the Christian response to the events of salvation that God has accomplished in his Son. We praise God for his becoming man and dwelling among us; for his death, which conquered sin; for his resurrection, which gives us new life; for his ascension to the right hand of the Father; and for sending the Holy Spirit to us at Pentecost (*CCC*, 2641). John Paul II says,

> To the extent that meditation on the mystery is attentive and profound, and to the extent that it is enlivened—from one *Hail Mary* to another—by love for Christ and for Mary, the glorification of the Trinity at the end of each decade, far from being a perfunctory conclusion, takes on its proper contemplative tone, raising the mind as it were to the heights of heaven, and enabling us in some way to relive the experience of [the Transfiguration], a foretaste of the contemplation yet to come: "It is good for us to be here!" (Luke 9:33). (*RVM*, 34)

In other words, when we attentively ponder the mysteries of salvation in the rosary, we cannot help but cry out in praise and thanksgiving, "Glory be to the Father, and to the Son, and to the Holy Spirit!" This is why John Paul II says the Glory Be should be given due importance in the rosary. He even suggests that when the rosary is recited publicly, this prayer of praise could be sung.

7. A Concluding Prayer: Life Application

It is common to say a brief prayer after each Glory Be. One popular practice is to recite the "Fatima Prayer": "O my Jesus, forgive us our sins, save us from the fires of hell, lead all souls to heaven, especially those in most need of thy mercy." In the reported apparition of Mary to three children in Fatima, Portugal, in 1917, she asked that this prayer be recited at the end of each decade.

John Paul II leaves open other possibilities for prayers at the close of each decade in harmony with local customs and diverse traditions. However, he suggests that contemplation of the mysteries could be expressed more fully "with a prayer for the fruits specific to that particular mystery" (*RVM*, 35). For example, at the end of the first joyful mystery (the annunciation), we could say, "Pray for us, Mary, that we may respond in obedient faith each day as you did." Or after the fourth sorrowful mystery (the carrying of the cross), we could say, "Pray for us, Mary, that we may carry our daily crosses in union with your son, Jesus." Or after the first glorious mystery (the Resurrection), we could say, "Pray for us, Mary, that we would share the peace of the Risen Christ with those around us."

8. The Beads as Symbols

John Paul II notes that even the rosary beads can play an important part in our devotion. On one hand, the beads liberate the mind from worrying about counting each Hail Mary. On the other hand, the beads carry a symbolism that can be helpful for contemplation.

First, he points out how all the beads converge on the crucifix, which represents the beginning and end point of the rosary's prayers. This can remind us that the entire Christian life is centered on Christ: "Everything begins from him, everything leads toward him, everything, through him, in the Holy Spirit, attains to the Father" (*RVM*, 36).

> "The 'sweet chain' of the rosary can free us from these fatal attractions."

Second, the pope notes that the beads symbolize a chain linking us to God as his servants. This is "a sweet chain" that is joined by the bonds of love. Our contemplation of Christ in the rosary can help draw us out of ourselves, out of our slavery to sin, and out of whatever addictions may keep us from living more fully with Christ.

Perhaps we struggle with traditional addictions, such as addictions to alcohol, pornography, sexual pleasure, or work. Or maybe we suffer from subtler addictions—to compliments, to pleasing others, to social media, or to being in control. The "sweet chain" of the rosary can free us from these fatal attractions by bringing our hearts into contact with something much more alluring: the infinite love of Jesus Christ (*RVM*, 36).

Third, the linking of the beads joined at the crucifix reminds us of our many relationships—family, friends, coworkers, neighbors, fellow Christians, the saints, and the angels—that are all intertwined in the common bond of Christ. When we pray the rosary, we can take time to pray for all these relationships, either in our hearts or by offering prayer intentions before we begin.

9. Opening and Closing

The Church offers diverse ways of beginning the rosary. One widely followed practice is to recite the Creed, one Our Father, three Hail

Marys, and a Glory Be as a prelude to the decades. This custom and others are intended to prepare the mind for contemplation of the mysteries.

At the end of the rosary, we pray for the intentions of the pope, embracing the needs of the Church as a whole. One common practice is to recite an Our Father, Hail Mary, and Glory Be for the Holy Father's intentions for the Church and for the world.

Finally, we recite a concluding prayer, such as the Hail, Holy Queen or the Litany of Mary, in thanksgiving for Mary's intercession for us throughout our contemplation of Christ in the rosary. John Paul II calls this a most fitting conclusion:

> Is it any wonder, then, that the soul feels the need, after saying [the rosary] and experiencing so profoundly the motherhood of Mary, to burst forth into praise of the Blessed Virgin, either in that splendid prayer the *Salve Regina* [Hail, Holy Queen] or in the Litany of Loreto? This is the crowning moment of an inner journey which has brought the faithful into living contact with the mystery of Christ and his Blessed Mother. (*RVM*, 37)

10. The Weekly Rhythm of the Mysteries

Technically speaking, the rosary consists of twenty decades in which all four sets of mysteries are contemplated: Joyful, Luminous, Sorrowful, and Glorious. The pope notes that the full rosary can be recited every day by contemplative priests and religious and by the sick and elderly, who often have more time at their disposal. However, since most people will be able to recite only part of the rosary each day, he recommends that we dedicate different days of the week to different sets of mysteries.

In previous practice, Monday and Thursday were dedicated to the Joyful Mysteries; Tuesday and Friday to the Sorrowful Mysteries; and Sunday, Wednesday, and Saturday to the Glorious Mysteries. With the introduction of the Mysteries of Light in 2002, John Paul II proposed a new weekly pattern.

The pope recommended that, since Saturday traditionally is associated with Mary, the Joyful Mysteries (in which Mary's presence is stressed more than in any other set of mysteries) be prayed on Saturday and Monday instead of Thursday and Monday. This frees Thursday for the Mysteries of Light—a fitting day for these mysteries, since they culminate with the institution of the Eucharist, which is celebrated on Holy Thursday in the Church's liturgical calendar.

Thus, while being open to other possibilities for distributing the mysteries, depending on particular pastoral needs, the pope proposed this weekly schedule for the Church:

Monday: Joyful Mysteries

Tuesday: Sorrowful Mysteries

Wednesday: Glorious Mysteries

Thursday: Luminous Mysteries

Friday: Sorrowful Mysteries

Saturday: Joyful Mysteries

Sunday: Glorious Mysteries

By reflecting on different mysteries throughout the week, the rosary gives each day its own spiritual color, like the liturgical colors that accent the different seasons of the Church's year. Week after week, we ponder anew the key moments in Christ's life—his birth, public ministry, death, and resurrection—and in these mysteries, we find the meaning of our own life's story—from birth to death, from joy to sorrow, from suffering to triumph, and ultimately, from this pilgrimage on earth to our hope in everlasting life. In this way, the rosary does indeed, as John Paul II says, "mark the rhythm of human life, bringing it into harmony with the 'rhythm' of God's own life" (*RVM*, 25, 38).

GROUP STUDY QUESTIONS

1. Why is the Glory Be a fitting finale for each decade of the rosary? How does this prayer relate to the mysteries we contemplate?

2. How do the beads aid your prayer of the rosary?

3. Pope St. John Paul II wrote, "It is clear...that many people will not be able to recite more than a part of the Rosary" every day, and hence comes the practice of reciting different sets of mysteries on different days. Some people might find it difficult to recite even five decades at one sitting—or kneeling. What are some ways of incorporating the rosary into a busy schedule?

4. The pope suggested that reciting different mysteries throughout the week "has the effect of giving the different days...a certain spiritual 'color'" (RVM, 38). How can the Joyful Mysteries color your Mondays and Saturdays? The Luminous, your Thursdays? The Sorrowful, your Tuesdays and Fridays? The Glorious, your Sundays?

CHAPTER EIGHT

Seeds for Contemplation:
Biblical Reflections on the Joyful Mysteries

In this first set of mysteries, we enter the joy radiating from the most unexpected event in the history of the world: God becoming man. We first see this joy in Gabriel's greeting of Mary, as the God of the universe is about to enter the human family in her womb. In the visitation, John the Baptist leaps for joy before the presence of Christ in Mary. In the nativity, the angels proclaim the "good news of a great joy" (Luke 2:10) to the shepherds who encounter the newborn Savior in Bethlehem.

St. John Paul II notes that the final two mysteries include a "joy mixed with drama," as they foreshadow the sorrow of Christ's suffering and death. In the presentation, the elderly Simeon rejoices in finally holding the Messiah in his arms, but he also foretells how the child will face intense opposition and how Mary too will suffer greatly. The last joyful mystery presents the twelve-year-old Christ going to Jerusalem for Passover and being lost for three days while doing his Father's will. This foreshadows his return to Jerusalem for Passover as an adult and his being lost when he is crucified on the cross, doing the will of his Father. As in his youth, Christ will be found again on the third day—this time in his resurrection.

The First Joyful Mystery

The Annunciation

LUKE 1:26–38

In the sixth month the angel Gabriel was sent from God to a city of Galilee named Nazareth, to a virgin betrothed to a man whose name was Joseph, of the house of David; and the virgin's name was Mary. And he came to her and said, "Hail, full of grace, the Lord is with you!" (Luke 1:26–28)

> "'Full of grace' is the name Mary possesses in the eyes of God"
> —St. John Paul II

Take a moment and imagine the quiet life of one young Jewish woman who from all outward appearances seems to be rather ordinary. She is a virgin betrothed to a man named Joseph, and she is probably in her early teen years. She lives in a small, insignificant village called Nazareth. Her name is Mary.

Suddenly, in the midst of her simple, routine life in Nazareth, an amazing event occurs: An angel of the Lord appears to her and says, "Hail, full of grace, the Lord is with you!" (Luke 1:28).

No angel has ever greeted anyone with such exalted language. Gabriel addresses Mary not by her personal name but with a title, "full of grace." As John Paul II commented, "'Full of grace' is the name Mary possesses in the eyes of God."[1]

In Greek, the word commonly translated "full of grace" (*kecharitomene*) indicates that Mary *already* is filled with God's saving grace. Indeed, God has prepared her for this defining moment. Chosen from the beginning of time to be the mother of the Savior, Mary has been shaped by God to be a pure, spotless sanctuary in which his Son will dwell. The all-holy Son of God will enter the world through the womb of a woman who is "full of grace."

The Lord Is with You!

Let's now ponder the angel's next words to Mary: "The Lord is with you!" For many Catholics, these words might seem like a routine greeting the priest says at Mass. However, for a Jewish woman of Mary's times, hearing "The Lord is with you!" would signal that she is called to play a crucial role in God's plan of salvation.

In the Old Testament, this phrase often was used when someone was being called for a special mission. For example, when Moses was called to lead the people out of Egypt, God told him, "I will be with you." When Joshua was called to lead Israel into the Promised Land, God said to him, "I will be with you." When Gideon was called to defend the people against the Philistines, when David was called to lead the kingdom, when Jeremiah the prophet was called to challenge the rulers in Jerusalem, they were all told that the Lord would be with them.

In each case, the person was commissioned to take on a difficult task with many risks and challenges. Often they felt inadequate and ill-prepared. Nevertheless, God challenged them to step outside their comfort zones and rely on him as never before. While they may not have felt ready for the job, they were given the one thing they needed most to carry out their task: The Lord would be with them.

Mary is about to be given one of the most important missions in Israel's history: to be the mother of the Messiah, who will bring salvation to the whole world. Such a role will not be easy. It will take her through many periods of trial, uncertainty, confusion, and suffering. Nevertheless, Gabriel tells Mary that she has the one thing she needs to be faithful to God's plan: The Lord is with her.

We need to hear that message too. How might God be asking you to rely on him more, to trust that the Lord is truly with *you* in whatever you might face in your life right now?

MOTHER OF THE KING

"And behold, you will conceive in your womb and bear a son, and you shall call his name Jesus. He will be great, and will be called the Son of the Most High; and the Lord God will give to him the throne of his father David, and he will reign over the house of Jacob for ever; and of his kingdom there will be no end" (Luke 1:31–33).

These words would have meant a lot to a young Jewish woman like Mary. For they recall the covenant promises God made to King David. In 2 Samuel 7, God told David that he would make his name "great" and establish "the throne of his kingdom for ever." David's royal descendants would be like God's son, and his "house" and "kingdom" "shall be made sure for ever" (2 Samuel 7:9–16).

For centuries, however, this Davidic dynasty stood in ruins. From the sixth century BC to Mary's time, practically, one foreign nation after another dominated the Jewish land, and no Davidic king ruled on the throne. Through the prophets, God promised the Jews that he would send them a new king, who would free them from their enemies and fulfill the promises he made to David. This king would be called the Messiah, the "anointed one." In Mary's day, the Jews were still waiting and wondering when God would send the Messiah to rescue them.

It is within this context that Gabriel tells Mary she will have a son to whom the Lord will give "the throne of his father David." And this son "will reign over the house of Jacob for ever; and of his kingdom there will be no end." Echoing the promises God made to David, Gabriel announces that the long-awaited everlasting kingdom is coming with this child!

Imagine how Mary must have felt when she realized that the Messiah-King was finally coming to Israel—and that she was chosen to be his mother! In her womb, she would carry all of Israel's deepest hopes and longings.

CONCEIVED BY THE HOLY SPIRIT

But how would this conception take place? Mary is a virgin and is not yet living with Joseph. She asks the angel, "How can this be, since I have no husband?" (Luke 1:34).

Now Gabriel delivers the most breathtaking part of his message: Mary will not have this child through natural means. No, miraculously, as a virgin, she will conceive through God's Holy Spirit. Thus, this child will not only be the messianic son of David; he will be the divine Son of God, coming from the Spirit and power of God himself: "The Holy Spirit will come upon you, and the power of the Most High will over-shadow you; therefore the child to be born will be called holy, the Son of God" (Luke 1:35).

> "The *Magnificat* tells us something about the *interior* journey Mary has been making."

What a mystery! The God of the entire universe will dwell in the virgin's womb. Mary will give birth to the one who gave her life. She will raise the child who is her own Savior. The Church's liturgical prayer expresses this mystery very well by referring to Mary as "Mother of her creator" and addressing her with the paradoxical title "daughter of your Son."[2]

How can this be? "For with God, nothing will be impossible," Gabriel says (Luke 1:37). And this message should inspire us to trust God more in our own lives. If God can work this miracle of miracles in Mary, certainly he can intervene in much smaller ways with us. Do we believe that God can help us with our trials, encourage us when we're down, comfort us in our suffering? Do we truly trust the Lord with our troubles, believing that "with God, nothing will be impossible"?

MARY'S "YES"

God is asking a lot of Mary. Consider all that has taken place in this brief encounter with Gabriel. First, she is told that she will be expecting a child. Next, she learns that this child will be Israel's long-awaited Messiah. Then, she discovers that her child will be the divine Son of God. And finally, she is told that she will conceive of this child as a virgin through the Holy Spirit of God. This is an awful lot to swallow in one short conversation with an angel!

What does this all mean? Where will this lead her? Does she feel ready to be a mother and, even more, ready to be the Mother of God? What will Joseph think when he finds out that she is pregnant? A lot of questions could have been racing through her mind.

According to St. Bernard of Clairvaux and others, all the angels and saints of the Old Testament would have been holding their breaths at this moment, wondering how the virgin would respond. Whatever she might have been thinking, the one thing we know for sure about Mary's reaction to God's extraordinary calling for her is that she has total trust. She says, "Behold, I am the handmaid of the Lord; let it be to me according to your word" (Luke 1:38).

John Paul II has pointed out that Mary's language ("let it be to me") indicates not a passive acceptance but an active embrace of God's plan for her.[3] Her words imply a wish or desire for God's will in her life. As such, Mary's "yes" serves as a model of faith for all believers.

We Christians sometimes submit to the Lord's will begrudgingly, as if it were something burdensome—a sacrifice we must make for the kingdom of God. ("Well, it's Lent again. I guess I have to give something up." "I better be kind to that annoying person because, as a Christian, I *have* to do that.") However, as we grow as God's children, we begin to realize that his plan for our lives always corresponds to our heart's deepest longings, to what will truly bring us fulfillment. Though at times very demanding and involving great sacrifices, God's will is not simply an ethical test we must pass or an external code of behavior to which we must submit. Ultimately, God's will is written on our hearts and is meant to lead us to a profound peace and happiness, even in the face of trials and sufferings.

May we, like Mary, actively desire God's will to be fulfilled in our lives. May we joyfully embrace his plan for us, not simply as a religious rule to obey but ultimately as the divine pathway to our hearts' deepest and most noble desires.

....

The Second Joyful Mystery
The Visitation
LUKE 1:39–56

In those days Mary arose and went with haste into the hill country, to a city of Judah, and she entered the house of Zechariah and greeted Elizabeth. And when Elizabeth heard the greeting of Mary, the babe leaped in her womb; and Elizabeth was filled with the Holy Spirit and she exclaimed with a loud cry, "Blessed are you among women, and blessed is the fruit of your womb! And why is this granted me, that the mother of my Lord should come to me?" (Luke 1:39–43)

At the annunciation, Mary learned that her kinswoman Elizabeth is miraculously expecting a child in her old age, "For with God nothing will be impossible" (Luke 1:37). Now Mary fervently desires to share in Elizabeth's joy and serve her during the last part of the pregnancy. She goes "with haste" to visit Elizabeth and then remains with her for three months.

Imagine the meeting of these two expectant mothers. What joy and excitement they have for each other. Elizabeth rushes out to greet Mary, saying, "Blessed are you among women, and blessed is the fruit of your womb!" (Luke 1:42). Filled with the Holy Spirit, Elizabeth recognizes that of all the women who have ever lived, Mary is most blessed, for the child in her womb is not any ordinary son but the Son of God himself.

In awe over this mystery, Elizabeth feels very privileged to be in the presence of the Lord dwelling in Mary. She says, "Why is this granted me, that the mother of my Lord should come to me?" Even the baby John the Baptist recognizes the presence of Jesus, leaping in Elizabeth's womb as soon as Mary arrives.

Do you approach God with the kind of joy that Elizabeth and John the Baptist exhibit—when you approach him in prayer? In the chapel? In the Eucharist?

Mary, Ark of the Covenant

This joy-filled reception of Mary and Jesus in the visitation is reminiscent of the way the ark of the covenant was welcomed in the Old Testament. As Israel's most important religious vessel, the ark carried three sacred items: the Ten Commandments; the staff of Aaron, the first high priest; and a jar containing manna, the heavenly bread that fed the Israelites for forty years in the desert (see Hebrews 9:4). Yet what made the ark most holy was God's presence, which overshadowed it in the form of a cloud (see Exodus 40:34).

When David became king, he wanted the ark to be brought to his capital city of Jerusalem. On the way there, the ark took a journey that is important for understanding the visitation scene. First the ark traveled to "the hill country of Judea," and it remained there in the "house of Obededom" for "three months" (see 2 Samuel 6:2, 11). When it eventually arrived in Jerusalem, there was a grand procession, with people shouting joyfully before the ark and David *leaping* before the Lord's presence (see 2 Samuel 6:12–16). The account also mentions that David's initial response to the ark was one of fear and wonder: "How can the ark of the Lord come to me?" (2 Samuel 6:9).

All this prefigures Mary's journey to visit Elizabeth. Like the ark of the covenant, Mary also travels "to the hill country…of Judea" and remains in a family's house, the "house of Zechariah," for "three months" (Luke 1:39–40, 56). Like David leaping before the ark, John the Baptist "leaped" in his mother's womb before Mary (Luke 1:41). And similar to David's awe-filled response before the ark of the covenant, Elizabeth's response to Mary is "And why is this granted me, that the mother of my Lord should come to me?" (Luke 1:43).

Finally, like the ark, Mary is greeted with shouts of joy, as Elizabeth "exclaimed with a loud cry" (Luke 1:42). The particular word Luke uses for "exclaimed" is used almost every time in the Greek Old Testament to portray the Levites exclaiming and praising God before the ark of the covenant.

"The same divine glory that once hovered over the ark of the covenant envelops these simple shepherds outside Bethlehem!"

These extensive parallels demonstrate beautifully that Luke is presenting Mary as a new ark of the covenant. What does this mean?

Just as God's presence once overshadowed the sanctuary, which housed the ark, so does the Holy Spirit now overshadow Mary (see Exodus 40:34–35; Luke 1:35). As the ark carried the Ten Commandments, so does Mary carry in her womb the one who has come to fulfill the Law (Matthew 5:17). As the ark carried the staff of the first high priest, so does Mary carry within her the last and true high priest, who will offer the perfect sacrifice to redeem the world (Hebrews 8:1–7). As the ark carried the heavenly bread called manna, so does Mary bear Jesus, who will call himself the true Bread of Life come down from heaven (John 6:48–51).

Most of all, as the ark of old bore God's presence to Israel, Mary bears the presence of God become man to the whole world. And being the new ark of the covenant she continues her role of bringing Christ into the world today through her powerful intercession for our lives.

THE *MAGNIFICAT*

What is going on inside Mary in these days after the annunciation? She certainly has had time to reflect on her profound vocation to serve as the mother of the world's Savior. During her long journey to Elizabeth's village, she probably pondered in her heart over and over again the words Gabriel spoke to her. And all the way to Judea, she knew she was no longer alone. She now carried in her womb the Son of God.

In the visitation scene, Mary breaks into hymn-like praise of God:

> My soul magnifies the Lord, and my spirit rejoices in God my Savior, for he has regarded the low estate of his handmaiden. For behold, henceforth all generations will call me blessed; for he who is mighty has done great things for me, and holy is his name. And his mercy is on those who fear him from generation to generation. (Luke 1:46–50)

This praise, commonly known as the *Magnificat*, tells us something about the *interior* journey Mary has been making. John Paul II says it represents the hidden depths of Mary's faith in these days.[4]

First Mary thanks the mighty God who has "done great things" for her. Viewing herself as a lowly servant, Mary humbly stands in awe before the fact that God has chosen her for such a high calling, to serve as the mother of the Messiah. However, in the second half of the *Magnificat*, Mary sees a connection between what God has done for her and what God wants to accomplish in the lives of all his people. She will bear the son who will do great things for *all* the lowly in Israel and in the world:

> He has shown strength with his arm, he has scattered the proud in the imagination of their hearts, he has put down the mighty from their thrones, and exalted those of low degree; he has filled the hungry with good things, and the rich he has sent empty away.

He has helped his servant Israel, in remembrance of his mercy, as he spoke to our fathers, to Abraham and to his posterity for ever. (Luke 1:51–55)

Here Mary views herself as the first recipient of the blessings God wishes to bring to all the faithful. Just as the Lord raised up Mary from her own lowliness because she was a faithful servant, so God wishes to exalt all the lowly and show mercy to all who fear him. Just as God has shown favor to his handmaiden Mary, so he will help "his servant Israel."

The *Magnificat* thus tells us that what God has done for this lowly woman of Nazareth, he will do for all who humbly serve him as Mary did. God will bless our faithfulness, look mercifully on our lowliness, and exalt us in our afflictions.

What are some ways God has exalted you and raised you up when you were down? Mary's example invites us to join her in thanking and praising the mighty God, who does "great things" for us. May we forever sing with her, "My soul magnifies the Lord!"

....

The Third Joyful Mystery
The Nativity
LUKE 2:1–20

In those days a decree went out from Caesar Augustus that all the world should be enrolled.... And all went to be enrolled, each to his own city. And Joseph also went up from Galilee, from the city of Nazareth, to Judea, to the city of David, which is called Bethlehem, because he was of the house and lineage of David, to be enrolled with Mary his betrothed, who was with child. And while they were there, the time came for her to be delivered. And she gave birth to her first-born son and wrapped him in swaddling cloths, and laid him in a manger, because there was no place for them in the inn. (Luke 2:1, 3–7)

Isn't this shocking? The Son of God enters the world with much hardship and poverty. Think about all Mary, Joseph, and the baby Jesus go through in this mystery. While Mary is in the last months of her pregnancy, she and Joseph are uprooted from their home in Nazareth and forced to travel to Bethlehem to be counted in a census—an oppressive tool that the Romans use to help collect taxes from the people.

> "'A sword will pierce through your soul also…. These words represent 'a second annunciation' to Mary."

Because "there was no place for them in the inn" (Luke 2:7), Mary experiences childbirth in an environment of extreme poverty. She cannot even give Jesus the basics of what any mother would want to offer a newborn baby. Instead a manger, a feeding trough for the animals, serves as an improvised cradle for the Son of God.[5]

How is this a mystery of joy?

The lowly beginnings of our Savior actually magnify how great God's love is for us. He loves us so much that he—the infinite, all-holy, all-powerful God—chooses to become one of us. He is willing to come to us even though practically everyone fails to give him a proper welcome, even though he must lie in a manger. In the presence of this utterly surprising great love, how can our hearts not be filled with joy?

Some early Christians saw Christ's humble beginnings as a foreshadowing of how he continues to meet us in the Eucharist. For example, St. Cyril of Alexandria said that when we sin, we fail to live out our dignity as humans made in the image of God, and we instead become like animals, living a life of self-gratification. Yet while animals feed from an ordinary manger, we as sinners approach Christ in a feeding trough that is much more substantial. Jesus feeds us not with hay but with his own Body and Blood in the Eucharist.[6]

Along these lines, it is most fitting that Jesus, the Eucharistic "bread of life" (John 6:35), is born in the city of Bethlehem, which in Hebrew literally means "house of bread."

THE GLORY OF THE LORD

"And in that region there were shepherds out in the field, keeping watch over their flock by night. And an angel of the Lord appeared to them, and the glory of the Lord shone around them, and they were filled with fear" (Luke 2:8–9).

In the fields, a group of shepherds tend their flock by night, unaware of the Savior child who has just been born in the city nearby. Suddenly, their ordinary lives are dramatically disrupted. Out of the darkness comes a dazzling brightness that encircles them, and they are afraid. It is "the glory of the Lord."

What is this glory that the shepherds behold? In the Old Testament, God's "glory" was the visible manifestation of his divine presence. It often came in the form of a cloud, covering the ark of the covenant or filling the temple in Jerusalem (see Exodus 40:34; 1 Kings 8:11; Ezekiel 10:4, 18). When the prophet Ezekiel had a vision of God's glory in the temple, he fell on his face in worship (Ezekiel 44:4).

The glory of the Lord, however, did not remain in the land of Israel forever. Shortly before Babylon invaded Jerusalem and destroyed the temple in 586 BC, God's glory left the sanctuary and the holy city because of the people's sinfulness (see Ezekiel 10–11). For hundreds of years, the Jewish people were without God's glory dwelling among them. Now on this night of Christ's birth, the same divine glory that once hovered over the ark of the covenant and filled the Holy of Holies envelops these simple shepherds in an open field outside Bethlehem!

Amid the brightness, an angel appears and assures them: "Be not afraid; for behold, I bring you good news of a great joy which will come to all the people; for to you is born this day in the city of David a Savior, who is Christ the Lord" (Luke 2:10–11).

Then a countless number of angels appear from heaven, praising God and saying, "Glory to God in the highest, and on earth peace among men with whom he is pleased!" (Luke 2:14). In their hymn of praise over the Bethlehem fields, these heavenly representatives joyfully recognize what seems to go unnoticed by almost everyone on earth: Today is born the Savior of the world, Christ the Lord!

THE SHEPHERDS' ENCOUNTER

Shepherds sat at the bottom of the social ladder in first-century Judaism. Often working for landowners, they received low wages. Religious Jews considered them dishonest and outside of God's covenant. Yet God chooses to announce Christ's birth not to the religious leaders in Jerusalem but to these lowly shepherds in the Bethlehem fields.

And the shepherds respond promptly to God's call. They receive the angel's message with enthusiastic faith, saying, "Let us go over to Bethlehem and see this thing that has happened, which the Lord has made known to us" (Luke 2:15). They go to the city "with haste" (Luke 2:16) and find what they have been looking for: Mary, Joseph, and the child Jesus lying in a manger, just as the angel has told them.

The shepherds marvel at their encounter with the newborn Christ and eagerly desire to tell others about him (see Luke 2:18). On this first Christmas night, they echo the angels' hymn of praise at the birth of Jesus: "And the shepherds returned, glorifying and praising God for all they had heard and seen" (Luke 2:20).

We too share in the angels' joyous announcement whenever we sing the *Gloria* at the beginning of Mass. Just as the angels welcomed the birth of Jesus in Bethlehem, singing "Glory to God," we prepare to welcome his coming in the Eucharist by saying: "Glory to God in the highest and peace to his people on earth."

How might the shepherds' example inspire us to share our joy over Jesus Christ with others?

....

The Presentation

LUKE 2:22–40

And when the time came for their purification according to the law of Moses, they brought him up to Jerusalem to present him to the Lord. (Luke 2:22)

Luke's account of Jesus's presentation in the temple is reminiscent of one of the most famous dedication scenes in the Old Testament: that of Samuel, who grew up to serve at the founding of the Davidic kingdom.

Like Mary and Joseph, Samuel's parents (Hannah and Elkanah) were devout Israelites who brought their child to the sanctuary and presented him to the Lord's service. They too encountered an elderly religious man (Eli) who blessed them (see 1 Samuel 2:20). The story of Samuel's beginnings also mentions women ministering outside the sanctuary (1 Samuel 2:22) and a statement about the growth of the child: "Now the boy Samuel continued to grow both in stature and in favor with the Lord and with men" (1 Samuel 2:26).

The parallels suggest that Luke is portraying Jesus as a new servant of the Lord. Just as Samuel was one of Israel's most important priests and prophets because of his key role in building the kingdom of David, so Jesus will go on to serve as the last and greatest of all the priests and prophets in Israel's history, for he will be the one to establish the everlasting kingdom of God.

GREAT EXPECTATIONS

"Now there was a man in Jerusalem whose name was Simeon, and this man was righteous and devout, looking for the consolation of Israel, and the Holy Spirit was upon him. And it had been revealed to him by the Holy Spirit that he should not see death before he had seen the Lord's Christ" (Luke 2:25–26).

Simeon is a model Jew. He is righteous and devout, and he waits for God to rescue his people Israel. Moreover, God has given Simeon a most extraordinary revelation: He will not die until he sees the Messiah. Patiently waiting and yearning to see the face of Christ, Simeon represents the many faithful Jews who for centuries longed for God to act in their lives, free them from their sufferings, and send them the Messiah-King.

Then one day it finally happens. Simeon is inspired by the Holy Spirit to visit the temple (see Luke 2:27). A man open to God's action in his life, Simeon responds to the Spirit's prompting. When he arrives at the temple, he encounters Joseph, Mary, and the child. What a moment this must be for Simeon!

> "In moments of spiritual aridity, we may feel like Mary and Joseph. We may feel that we have lost Christ."

Simeon's example invites us to consider how we respond to the Spirit's promptings. When we sense we should stop by the chapel, say sorry to our spouse, stop looking at something that appears on our screen, or spend some time with a certain child, how do we respond? Do we take these promptings seriously?

Imagine if Simeon had ignored the prompting to go to the temple, saying to himself, "I'm too busy today," or, "Oh, that's not a big deal. I'll visit the temple another time." He would have missed the encounter of a lifetime. What might we miss if we fail to respond when the Spirit knocks on the door of our hearts?

But Simeon does go. And when he sees the baby Jesus, he takes the child in his arms and blesses God, saying: "Lord, now let your servant depart in peace, according to your word; for my eyes have seen your salvation which you have prepared in the presence of all peoples, a light for revelation to the Gentiles, and for glory to your people Israel" (Luke 2:29–32).

After years of longing for God to act, Simeon can finally go to his rest. He has seen with his own eyes what God does for those who patiently wait on the Lord. He has held in his own arms the hopes of all of Israel. In this child, God has been faithful to his promises and will rescue his people.

A Sword Will Pierce Your Soul Also

The joy radiating throughout this scene suddenly turns to sorrow. After praising God for sending the Savior, Simeon turns to Mary and utters the following prophecy: "Behold, this child is set for the fall and rising of many in Israel, and for a sign that is spoken against (and a sword will pierce through your own soul also), that thoughts out of many hearts may be revealed" (Luke 2:34–35).

With these words, Mary catches a glimpse of the difficult road that lies ahead. Her son's future will be full of conflict and turmoil. Simeon first says the child "is set for the fall and rising of many in Israel." This foreshadows how the poor and outcast of Jesus's day will be exalted in his ministry, while many of the Jewish leaders will reject him and exclude themselves from his kingdom. Simeon also says the child will be "a sign that is spoken against," meaning that Jesus will face hostile opposition, even from his own people.

Most devastating is the image of the "sword," which signifies bloodshed and death. This points forward to how Jesus eventually will suffer bloodshed on the cross and be killed by his enemies.

By saying to Mary "a sword will pierce *through your soul also*," Simeon emphasizes the effects Christ's sufferings will have in her life. John Paul II says these words represent "a second annunciation" to Mary, because they show her more clearly how her initial "yes" to God will be lived out. She will see her son misunderstood and plotted against throughout his public ministry and eventually killed by his enemies in Jerusalem.[7]

Consider the heroic faith of Mary in those dark moments on Good Friday. Gabriel originally told her that she would be the mother of Israel's Messiah, the mother of the one whose kingdom would have no end. Yet as John Paul II points out, at the foot of the cross, Mary will be a witness, from a human perspective, to the negation of those words. Humanly speaking, the cross is anything but royal splendor; it is tragedy and defeat, especially for the mother who can do nothing but helplessly watch her son die a horrible death.

How great then must be Mary's trust as she enters what could be called a "spiritual crucifixion," letting go of her son and abandoning herself to God's care.[8] The trials at Calvary are foreshadowed in this scene from Christ's infancy with Simeon's prophetic warning to Mary, "A sword will pierce through your soul also."

....

The Fifth Joyful Mystery
The Finding of the Child Jesus in the Temple
LUKE 2:41–52

Supposing him to be in the company they went a day's journey, and they sought him among their kinsfolk and acquaintances; and when they did not find him, they returned to Jerusalem, seeking him. (Luke 2:44)

Imagine what Mary and Joseph are experiencing. When making a pilgrimage to Jerusalem for a feast like Passover, it was common for Jews to travel in large caravans made up of extended family members and friends. Assuming Jesus is with one of their kinsfolk, Mary and Joseph go a whole day's journey without realizing that their child is missing.

But at the end of the day, they cannot find Jesus. They search for him frantically throughout the caravan. They ask their friends and relatives. No one has seen him.

Now they return to Jerusalem. After looking through the city, they enter the temple on the third day and find Jesus talking with the Jewish rabbis, stunning them with his knowledge. Mary approaches Jesus and says to him, "Son, why have you treated us so? Behold, your father and I have been looking for you anxiously" (Luke 2:48).

Jesus responds, "How is it that you sought me? Did you not know that I must be in *my Father's house?* [emphasis added]" This expression can be translated "my Father's affairs" or "my Father's business" (Luke 2:49). At a young age, Jesus already is emphasizing that he must be busy doing the will of his heavenly Father, even if it means that those he loves will suffer. Mary and Joseph, however, are bewildered by their son's statement: "They did not understand the saying which he spoke to them" (Luke 2:50).

A Preview to Good Friday

They lost Jesus. They could not find him for three days. They did not understand.

This scene from the childhood of Jesus prefigures what will take place at the climax of his ministry as an adult. In the last days of his life, Jesus will make another pilgrimage to Jerusalem for the Feast of Passover. There in the holy city, he will enter the temple and engage the Jewish teachers in the sanctuary. He will amaze many with his wisdom, just as he did in his youth.

On this later occasion, however, the astonishment will lead to his demise, as the Jerusalem leaders plot his death. Once again, Jesus will be taken away from his mother, this time to be crucified on Calvary. And standing below the cross, Mary, as would any mother, will feel the pains of not fully understanding how her son could suffer such a tragic death. Yet at the same time, Mary will trust that Jesus must be about his Father's affairs, fulfilling the will of the Father. And just as Mary found

Jesus on the third day in Jerusalem as a child, she will find him again on the third day when he rises from the dead on Easter morning.

LOST AND FOUND

The Catholic theologian Romano Guardini once said that Mary and Joseph's experience in this scene sometimes repeats itself spiritually in the life of the Christian:

> At first, Christ is the center; our faith in Him is firm and loving. But then He disappears for a while, suddenly and apparently without the slightest reason. A remoteness has been created. A void is formed. We feel forsaken. Faith seems folly…. Everything becomes heavy, wearisome, and senseless. We must walk alone and seek. But one day we find Christ again—and it is in such circumstances that the power of the Father's will becomes evident to us.[9]

In moments of spiritual aridity, we may feel like Mary and Joseph. We may feel that we have lost Christ. Our prayer seems dry and point-less. Our pious practices seem like chores. We search for him everywhere through all our familiar methods of prayer and devotion, but he is nowhere to be found. We do not understand.

Eventually, however, we find him again. And then we discover that Jesus has been with us all along. By withdrawing the pleasant consolations that initially attracted us to the spiritual life, Jesus invites us to come to him for *who* he is—not for the good feelings he may give us in prayer. In doing so, he calls us to a deeper level of trust and an even more intimate communion with him. While he may seem lost to us, he really is doing his Father's business in the interior temples of our souls.

GROUP STUDY QUESTIONS

1. "To meditate upon the 'joyful' mysteries…is to enter into the ulti-mate causes and the deepest meaning of Christian joy" (*RVM*, 20).

How might the Joyful Mysteries inspire your observance of Advent? Of Christmas? Of Ordinary Time?

2. What virtues do the Joyful Mysteries inspire you to develop?

3. How do Old Testament events, places, and things deepen your understanding of these Joyful Mysteries?

4. In the Magnificat, Mary says, "His mercy is on those who fear him from generation to generation" (Luke 1:50). Thus Mary assures us that we too are recipients of God's regard. What blessings has God granted you? What qualities of Mary can you adopt in order to make you more aware of the "great things" God has for you?

5. "Be not afraid," the angel told the shepherds on Christmas night (Luke 2:10). Pope St. John Paul II echoed this theme in his inauguration homily: "Brothers and sisters, do not be afraid to welcome Christ and accept his power.... Do not be afraid. Open wide the doors for Christ.... Do not be afraid."[10] What credibility do the angel and the pope have in delivering these messages? How might Mary and this pope saint help you maintain courage to face challenges in your life?

6. What is the "Father's business" in your soul right now? How can you cooperate with that work?

CHAPTER NINE

Seeds for Contemplation: Biblical Reflections on the Luminous Mysteries

The Luminous Mysteries are all about the light of Christ overcoming the darkness, shining in the places we least expect.

Take, for example, Christ's baptism in the Jordan in the first luminous mystery. Jesus, the sinless one, surprisingly enters the same waters of repentance that sinners have entered. And it is precisely in meeting the people in their act of repentance that his divine light is manifested: The heavens open, and the Spirit descends upon him, while the Father's voice declares, "This is my beloved Son, with whom I am well pleased" (Matthew 3:17).

In the second mystery, the wedding at Cana, the light of Christ is revealed in the water from the Jewish purification jars, which are used at the feast for ritual handwashing or utensil cleaning. Jesus transforms the water from these jars into an abundance of good wine, performing his first miracle. This act symbolizes what Christ wants to do in all our hearts. He wants his light to fall on the dirty jars in our lives—our weaknesses, fears, wounds, and sins—so that they may be transformed with new life by his grace.

In the third mystery, the proclamation of the kingdom, John Paul II suggests that we focus on Christ's call to conversion and his forgiveness for those who humbly approach him. Once again, in this mystery we see Christ's light shining in the least expected places: on sinners, tax collectors, lepers, prostitutes, pagans, and all the other social and religious outcasts of the day. They hear his call to repent and receive his forgiveness.

In the fourth luminous mystery, the Transfiguration, Christ's light is manifested at a most unusual time. Just after Jesus tells the apostles the startling news that he must go to Jerusalem to suffer and be crucified, he goes up a mountain with Peter, James, and John and allows them to witness his divine glory. By displaying his glory just after predicting his passion, the Transfiguration scene foreshadows how the glory of the Savior is revealed most fully not in worldly triumph but in his sacrificial love on the cross.

Similarly, the final mystery, the institution of the Eucharist, is placed in the context of Christ's suffering. During the Last Supper, his enemies plot his arrest, and one of his own apostles leaves the table to go betray him. Yet, here as the drama of his passion and death is about to unfold, Jesus leaves us the profound gift of himself in the Eucharist. Under the appearances of bread and wine, Christ's Body and Blood are made truly present to us today in the Mass. In this Holy Communion, the divine light of Christ shines most intimately in the caverns of our souls, drawing us into deeper unity with Our Lord.

....

The First Luminous Mystery
Christ's Baptism in the Jordan
MATTHEW 3:13–17; MARK 1:9–11; LUKE 3:21–22

John the baptizer appeared in the wilderness, preaching a baptism of repentance for the forgiveness of sins. And there went out to him all the country of Judea, and all the people of Jerusalem; and they were baptized by him in the river Jordan, confessing their sins. (Mark 1:4–5)

The desert wilderness around the Jordan River does not seem to be the ideal place to start a movement. To get there from Jerusalem, we would have to travel several hours through rugged terrain and desert heat. Upon arrival, we would find ourselves at the lowest point on the face of the earth—some twelve hundred feet below sea level. From a modern perspective, we might say that the Jordan River basin lies in the middle of nowhere.

Imagine being a traveler who just happens to be passing through this barren place at this time. Suddenly, to your great surprise, you see multitudes of people from all over Judea gathering around a man wearing a garment of camel hair and a leather girdle around his waist (Matthew 3:4). His name is John, and he calls religious groups such as the Sadducees and Pharisees, as well as tax collectors, soldiers, and prostitutes, to repent and participate in his ritual of baptism in the Jordan River (see Matthew 3:7; 21:32; Luke 3:10–14).

"He chose the Jordan River because he wanted to send a powerful message: The new exodus is here."

What is this all about? And why would so many people come out here in the wilderness just to be baptized in the Jordan? Isn't there water in Jerusalem and in Galilee?

No Ordinary River

For the Jews, the Jordan River was not any ordinary water source. It was a river that symbolized new beginnings. Elijah the prophet was taken up to heaven at the Jordan. Elisha, his successor, began his prophetic ministry at this same spot. Naaman the Syrian was cured of his leprosy at this river (see 2 Kings 5:1–19).

However, what made the Jordan stand out most for the Jews was its association with the Exodus story. After fleeing from slavery in Egypt and wandering in the desert for forty years, the Israelites finally entered the Promised Land by passing through the Jordan River. Thus, the crossing of the Jordan represents the climax of the Exodus (see Joshua 3:14–17).

Jews in the first century were hoping for a new type of exodus in their lives. In fact, the prophets used the Exodus story as an image for what God would do in the messianic age. They foretold that one day, God would free the people from their enemies, just as he once liberated their ancestors from Pharaoh in Egypt. Jews in John's day longed for these prophecies to be fulfilled. They believed God eventually would send Israel a new king, a Messiah, who would rescue them from their present-day oppressors and bring about the new exodus.

This helps explain why John chose to baptize in the Jordan. Although he could have baptized in many other locations, he chose the Jordan River because he wanted to send a powerful message: The new exodus is here. In inviting people to travel out into the desert, go down into the waters of the Jordan, and reenter the land, John was having the people reenact the Exodus story. Such a symbolic action expressed hope that the final great exodus was about to take place. It is no wonder there was so much enthusiasm and expectation surrounding John's movement!

The Baptism of the Sinless One

Now imagine that you stay and watch this movement for a bit. While crowds come to John to be baptized, you notice someone new approaching. He gets in line with the repentant sinners. It's Jesus, the Messiah. No one but John recognizes him.

Understandably, John does not feel worthy to baptize the Messiah. He humbly acknowledges his subordinate role of preparing the way for Jesus: "I need to be baptized by you, and do you come to me?" (Matthew 3:14). Nevertheless, Jesus insists: "Let it be so now; for thus it is fitting for us to fulfill all righteousness" (Matthew 3:15).

One can appreciate John's trepidation. After all, who would be worthy to baptize the Son of God? And there is an even more puzzling question: *Why* would Jesus need to be baptized in the first place? If John's baptism symbolizes repentance of sins and Jesus is sinless, why does he undergo this ritual?

Certainly, Jesus does not *need* baptism or repentance, but he participates in this ritual in order to demonstrate his solidarity with Israel and all humanity. By going into the same waters that the repentant are entering, he shows us that he has come to unite himself to sinners so that they may be restored in him to the Father. In this action at the beginning of his messianic mission, Jesus foreshadows how he will bear the sins of all the world on the cross at the culmination of his public ministry.

The *Catechism* makes this point when explaining Christ's baptism: "He allows himself to be numbered among sinners; he is already 'the Lamb of God, who takes away the sins of the world.' Already he is anticipating the 'baptism' of his bloody death" (*CCC*, 536).

THE HEAVENS OPEN

At the moment of his baptism, we watch Jesus step into the water and pray. Then, as he comes out of the water, "immediately he saw the heavens opened and the Spirit descending upon him like a dove; and a voice came from heaven, 'You are my beloved Son; with you I am well pleased'" (Mark 1:10–11).

"The Spirit descending like a dove" recalls how God's Spirit hovered over the waters at the start of creation (see Genesis 1:2). It also brings to mind how Noah sent out a dove that hovered over the waters of the renewed creation after the Flood (Genesis 8:10–12). Now that same Spirit falls on Jesus in the waters of the Jordan and thus signals another new beginning for the world: The broken, divided human family is about to be recreated in the one family of God through Christ's Holy Spirit.

This biblical theme of God's Spirit coming upon the waters to renew all creation helps us to understand what really happens in the sacrament of baptism today. In the waters of baptism, we encounter that same Holy Spirit, and he once again comes to bring new life. At the moment of baptism, God's Spirit fills our souls and transforms us with his supernatural life. We truly become new creations (see 2 Corinthians 5:17; Galatians 6:15), adopted sons and daughters of God (Galatians 3:15–4:7). As a result of Christ's Spirit dwelling in our hearts, the heavenly Father now can say to us what he first said to Jesus at the Jordan, "You are my beloved Son."

THE LORD'S SERVANT

Finally, while the voice from heaven exalts Christ as the beloved Son in whom the Father is well pleased, it also foreshadows the painful road the Son must travel. Let us consider how these words from heaven recall a prophecy in the Old Testament about the servant of the Lord.

God foretold through Isaiah that he would send a faithful servant to fulfill his plan of salvation. God would rejoice in this servant, saying: "*Behold, my servant,* whom I uphold, my chosen, *in whom my soul delights*; I have put *my Spirit upon him*" (Isaiah 42:1, italics added). This servant of the Lord would reunite all of Israel (see Isaiah 49:5) and be a light to all the nations (Isaiah 42:6; 49:6). Yet this servant would accomplish God's redemptive plan through much suffering for our sins (Isaiah 53).

At Christ's baptism, the Spirit descends on Jesus, and the voice from heaven says: "You are my beloved Son; with you I am well pleased." These words echo Isaiah's prophecy about the servant of the Lord—the servant in whom the Father delights and on whom the Spirit rests. Jesus is thus presented as God's faithful servant who will be a light to all the world.

This servant was expected to endure great suffering on account of our sins. Therefore, while this opening scene of Christ's public life exalts him as the Son of God anointed by the Holy Spirit, it also subtly foreshadows how Jesus will endure great affliction for our sins as the suffering servant from Isaiah. Indeed, Christ's messianic mission will culminate in his sacrifice on the cross.

....

The Second Luminous Mystery
The Wedding Feast at Cana
JOHN 2:1–11

On the third day there was a marriage at Cana in Galilee, and the mother of Jesus was there; Jesus also was invited to the marriage, with his disciples. When the wine failed, the mother of Jesus said to him, "They have no wine." (John 2:1–3)

Imagine the pain and embarrassment the newlyweds would have felt over running out of wine at their own wedding feast. Noticing the crisis at hand and moved with pity for them, Mary rushes to bring the problem to Jesus's attention. St. Thomas Aquinas says we should note Mary's kindness and mercy in this scene: "For it is a quality of mercy to regard another's distress as one's own, because to be merciful is to have a heart distressed at the distress of another."[1]

John Paul II sees in this act of kindness a pattern for Mary's continued concern over the needs of all Christians. Just as Mary intercedes on behalf of the couple at Cana, so she continues to bring our needs before her son. Thus, this scene serves as an example of *"Mary's solicitude for human beings*, her coming to them in the wide variety of their wants and needs" and "bringing those needs within the radius of Christ's messianic mission."[2]

Most significantly, we also see that Mary has tremendous faith in her son. Jesus is just a guest; he does not have any wine at his disposal. Up to this point, he has not performed any miracles. Therefore, from a natural perspective, Mary has no reason to ask him to help.

Still, when Mary notices that the wine has run out, her first instinct is to turn to Jesus. Such an unusual request only makes sense if she expects Jesus to work some extraordinary sign. Though she has yet to see her son work a single miracle, she has faith in his supernatural power and believes that he can help.

"WOMAN"

"And Jesus said to her, 'O woman, what have you to do with me? My hour has not yet come'" (John 2:4).

At first glance, Jesus seems a little harsh. His response to Mary's request appears to be disrespectful, perhaps even a rebuke, as if he were pushing his mother away. After all, how many children would dare to call their own mother "woman"?

However, as we continue reading the story, we see that Jesus is not in any way rejecting his mother or her request. Whatever the address "woman" may mean, Mary does not seem to interpret it negatively. Her response, in fact, suggests that she believes he will solve the problem promptly. She tells the servants, "Do whatever he tells you" (John 2:5).

Moreover, Jesus does not reject Mary's request but responds to it favorably by changing the water to wine. So whatever this puzzling title "woman" may mean, it cannot be something harsh and negative.

When this passage is considered within the wider context of John's Gospel, the title "woman" takes on greater meaning. The Gospel of John begins the story of Jesus against the backdrop of the story of creation. The opening line of the Gospel is "In the beginning was the Word" (John 1:1)—a phrase taken right from the start of the creation story in Genesis 1:1: "In the beginning God created the heavens and the earth." John's Gospel then goes on to speak of creation, life, light, and light shining in the darkness—all images from the creation story (see John 1:1–5). By using this Genesis imagery, John is announcing that the arrival of Jesus marks a new beginning for the world. The coming of Christ will bring about a renewal of creation, which has been disrupted by sin.

Some commentators also point out that John's Gospel begins with a series of seven days, which establishes a new creation week. In the first chapter, John sets up a succession of four days, starting with John 1:1, "In the beginning." John 1:29 says, "the next day," marking day number two. John 1:35 and 1:43 also say, "the next day," accounting for days three and four. Then the second chapter begins: "*On the third day* there was a marriage at Cana in Galilee" (John 2:1). The third day after the fourth day would represent the seventh day in John's Gospel. Thus, the wedding feast at Cana takes place at the culmination of the new creation week in the Gospel of John, the seventh day.

A New Eve

Now we are prepared to understand more about the meaning of Jesus's response to Mary in this scene. At the climax of this new creation week, Jesus calls his mother "woman." Understood within the context of the Genesis background, the title "woman" would recall the woman of Genesis, Eve (see Genesis 2:23). In this sense, Mary can be seen as a new Eve—a perspective that Christians from as early as the second century have held. Whereas the first Eve cooperated in the fall of humanity, Mary, the new Eve, cooperates in the redemption of the human family. As St. Irenaeus said, "The knot of Eve's disobedience was untied through the obedience of Mary. For what the virgin Eve had tied through unbelief, the Virgin set free through faith."[3]

As the faithful new Eve, Mary tells the servants, "Do whatever he tells you" (John 2:5). Here we see Mary serving as a spokeswoman for her son's will, exhorting others to trust in Jesus's commands. Indeed, following Jesus's instructions requires a lot of trust on the servants' part, because he asks them to do something very strange with the six stone jars for the Jewish rites of purification that are standing there. These jars probably would have been used at the feast for ritual handwashing or cleansing of utensils (see Mark 7:3–4). What is astounding is that Jesus commands the servants to fill these jars with water and bring some of their contents to the steward of the feast.

However odd such a request might seem and despite their uncertainty about how this will resolve the problem, the servants obediently carry out Jesus's desire. Imagine their trepidation as they watch their boss taste the water. And imagine their great surprise when they witness his joyful response. Not knowing where this liquid came from, the steward calls the bridegroom and says to him, "Every man serves the good wine first; and when men have drunk freely, then the poor wine; but you have kept the good wine until now" (John 2:10).

> "What Christ has done in those dirty purification jars he wishes to do in each of us: *cleanse us of our sins and transform us into 'good wine'.*"

In this first of Christ's miracles, the servants discover the amazing things that happen when people trust Jesus. John Paul II comments on how Mary's command, "Do whatever he tells you," continues to have meaning for our lives today: "It is an exhortation to trust without hesitation, especially when one does not understand the meaning or benefit of what Christ asks."[4] Thus we are called to have faith like that of the servants, trusting Christ's will for our lives and doing whatever he tells us, even when the pathway may be unclear or the outcome uncertain.

The Good Wine

"This, the first of his signs, Jesus did at Cana in Galilee, and manifested his glory; and his disciples believed in him" (John 2:11).

This first of Jesus's miracles sets the tone for understanding his entire public ministry. The water being transformed into "good wine" can symbolize the movement from the old covenant to the new. On one hand, water from the Jewish rites of purification would serve as a symbol of the old covenant, which is reaching its culmination in Christ. On the other hand, the prophets used the image of overflowing wine to symbolize the blessings God would bestow on Israel in the messianic age (see Isaiah 25:6; Jeremiah 31:12; Joel 3:18; Amos 9:13).

Therefore, Jesus's miracle of turning the water from the ritual cleansing jars into an overabundance of wine expresses the fact that the new covenant era is here. Furthermore, what Christ has done in those dirty purification jars he wishes to do in each of us: *cleanse us* of our sins and *transform us* into "good wine."

....

The Third Luminous Mystery
The Proclamation of the Kingdom
MARK 1:14–15; MATTHEW 6:25–27; LUKE 15:11–24

From that time Jesus began to preach, saying, "Repent, for the kingdom of eaven is at hand." (Matthew 4:17)

This third mystery of light offers much to contemplate, for it encompasses practically the entirety of Christ's public ministry. In his apostolic letter on the rosary, John Paul II suggests two themes in particular for us to ponder when praying this mystery: Christ's call to conversion and his forgiving the sins of those who come to him in humble trust.

While numerous scenes from Christ's proclamation of the kingdom could be considered, this reflection will focus on just a few passages that exemplify the themes the pope recommended. Let us begin by considering the call to conversion.

THE CALL TO CONVERSION

"Jesus came into Galilee, preaching the gospel of God, and saying, 'The time is fulfilled, and the kingdom of God is at hand; repent, and believe in the gospel'" (Mark 1:14–15).

One basic meaning of *conversion* is "to turn." Throughout the Bible, when God calls his people to repentance, he is inviting them to reorient their lives—to turn away from sin and *turn back* to him. This involves an honest evaluation of one's life. We must ask, "What is truly at the center of my life? Do I live as if God is at the very center of all I desire, all I strive for, all I do? Or is there something else—such as wealth, status, achievement, approval, or pleasure—that I am hoping will bring me fulfillment, security, and happiness?"

One passage from Christ's proclamation of the kingdom that challenges us to make such a self-assessment and to realign our lives accordingly comes from the Sermon on the Mount:

> Therefore I tell you, do not be anxious about your life, what you shall eat or what you shall drink, nor about your body, what you shall put on. Is not life more than food, and the body more than clothing? Look at the birds of the air: they neither sow nor reap nor gather into barns, and yet your heavenly Father feeds them. Are you not of more value than they? And which of you by being anxious can add one cubit to his span of life?... Therefore do not be anxious, saying, "What shall we eat?" or "What shall we drink?" or "What shall we wear?" For the Gentiles seek all these things; and your heavenly Father knows that you need them all. But seek first his kingdom and his righteousness, and all these things shall be yours as well. (Matthew 6:25–33)

One helpful way to discern what we put at the center of our lives is to consider what we worry about. That is what Jesus challenges us to ponder in these verses. It is as if he were telling us, "Do not be anxious saying, 'What shall we eat? What shall we drink? How will we make the car payment? What does she think of me? How will I get everything done this week? Did I leave a good impression?'" When something causes us great anxiety or worry, it is often a sign that we are not seeking first Christ's kingdom. We have allowed something other than God to move to the center of our lives. We are in need of a realignment.

Seeking First the Kingdom

It is important to note that Jesus does not say that these worldly concerns are bad. God certainly wants us to pay the bills, strive for excellence in our work, find good friendships, and have food on the table. "Your heavenly Father knows that you need them all," Jesus says. It is just that these things cannot sustain us at the center of our being, for they cannot make us truly happy. When we treat

> "When something causes us great anxiety or worry; it is often a sign that we are not seeking first Christ's kingdom."

finite pleasures, successes, possessions, or honors like an infinite god, a source of lasting fulfillment and security, they will fall short every time. When they creep into the center, they will leave us feeling empty, frustrated, and very anxious about our lives.

That is why Jesus goes on to say, "But seek first his kingdom and his righteousness, and all these things shall be yours as well" (Matthew 6:33). If God's will is truly our first priority, the other areas of our lives tend to fall into place, because they are centered on the one sure foundation. When we put our trust in the one who knows our needs far better than we do, all our desires and longings find a certain harmony, since they are centered around Christ. Thus, the call to conversion involves an ongoing turning back to God, as we entrust more of our lives to him and desire to live with him at the center of our hearts.

Forgiveness of Sins

In this mystery of the rosary, John Paul II also suggests that we contemplate Christ's forgiving the sins of those who come to him in humble trust. This second theme flows from the first, the call to conversion. While discerning what keeps us from living with Christ at the center of our lives, we can encounter a difficult moment in discovering the hard truth about ourselves—the truth about how proud, self-centered, envious, cowardly, lustful, or critical we really are. Yet it is precisely in this humbling realization of our own tragic flaws and weaknesses that God meets us with his mercy and gives the sinner hope.

St. Bernard of Clairvaux once said that the stark reality of this painful truth about ourselves would be intolerable without the grace of God's mercy. That is why Bernard would not allow himself to focus exclusively on the fact of his own sinfulness but would look at his broken condition in the light of God's mercy: "As for me, as long as I look at myself, my eye is filled with bitterness. But if I look up and fix my eyes on the aid of the divine mercy, this happy vision of God soon tempers the bitter vision of myself."[5]

This is how the woman caught in adultery must have felt. The scribes and Pharisees throw her in front of Jesus, to use her as a test case to trap him. They ask Jesus if she should be stoned, since the Law of Moses prescribes such a penalty for women who commit adultery (see John 8:2–11). Roman law, however, prohibits the Jews from exacting capital punishment on their own. If Jesus agrees to stone her, he will be in trouble with the Romans. If he tells them not to stone her, they will accuse him of being unfaithful to the Law of Moses. Jesus is being set up, and there does not seem to be any way to answer their question without facing much hostility.

Jesus, however, not only avoids the trap but takes the conversation to a completely new level. The scribes and Pharisees focus on a legal issue, while Jesus focuses on the person. Jesus challenges them to consider the way of forgiveness instead of the path of condemnation:

And as they continued to ask him, he stood up and said to them, "Let him who is without sin among you be the first to throw a stone at her."... But when they heard it, they went away, one by one, beginning with the eldest, and Jesus was left alone with the woman standing before him. Jesus looked up and said to her, "Woman, where are they? Has no one condemned you?" She said, "No one, Lord." And Jesus said, "Neither do I condemn you; go, and do not sin again." (John 8:7, 9–11)

Encountering Mercy

Accused, shamed, and used as a pawn in the Pharisees' dispute with Jesus, the woman stands humiliated before the crowd. Put yourself in her situation. What is your most embarrassing hidden sin? Imagine that weakness coming out into the open. Your friends, family, colleagues all know. How would *you* feel? Afraid. Ashamed. Angry. The woman probably has a lot of self-condemnation as well. I'm sure she is, in a sense, throwing stones at herself before anyone in the crowd does.

But just at this moment, Jesus does the most unexpected thing. He doesn't condemn the woman. Even though she has committed a serious sin, Jesus still loves her. He comes to offer mercy. He says to the crowd: "Let him who is without sin among you be the first to throw a stone at her." None of the scribes and Pharisees condemn her, and neither does Jesus.

While Jesus does not overlook the woman's adultery (he tells her, "Do not sin again"), neither does he come as a judge to evaluate the legal fact of her sin. Yes, she has broken the moral law, and yes, she has sinned. But Jesus focuses on the person, not the legal facts, and he comes to offer her his mercy. He gives her the chance to turn back to God and sin no more.

Jesus does the same with us. No matter what we've done in the past and no matter what we might be struggling with right now, Jesus comes to us sinners not as a harsh prosecuting attorney, suspecting the worst in our actions, doubting our motives, and ready to condemn. Rather, he comes as our Savior, offering us understanding, forgiveness, and the opportunity to start over again—as long as we turn back to him at the center of our lives.

It is no wonder that John Paul II mentions the sacrament of reconciliation when discussing this third luminous mystery, for it is in this sacrament that the kingdom's call to conversion and ministry of mercy are most fully realized (*RVM*, 21). In humbly recognizing the truth of our failings before God, we begin the process of conversion. When we confess our sins in the sacrament of reconciliation, we can experience the Father's forgiveness, as well as Jesus's powerful grace to help us turn and live with him again at the center of our lives.

Jesus is waiting for you in this powerful sacrament. He's waiting for you to get that certain thing off your chest, to stop rationalizing what you've done, to stop condemning yourself, and simply to come and experience his love, forgiveness, and healing power in this beautiful sacrament of mercy.

· ·

The Fourth Luminous Mystery
The Transfiguration
MATTHEW 17:1–8

He was transfigured before them, and his face shone like the sun. (Matthew 17:2)

Imagine being on top of that mountain when Jesus was transfigured. You've witnessed Jesus's preaching and healing power throughout his public ministry, but up until this point, the fullness of Christ's glory has been veiled. Now you, along with Peter, James, and John, catch a glimpse of that glory as you witness Jesus's face shining like the sun and his garments becoming a dazzling white.

You also notice Jesus speaking with two leading men from Israelite history, who together represent the entire old covenant: Moses, who symbolizes the Law, and Elijah, who symbolizes the prophets. Amid this conversation, a bright cloud filled with God's glory suddenly overshadows them, and the apostles hear a heavenly voice saying, "This is my beloved Son with whom I am well pleased; listen to him" (Matthew 17:5).

What is the purpose behind this spectacular display of Jesus's glory? Why is Jesus transfigured at this point in his public ministry? The context surrounding this scene helps us to appreciate the significance of this point in Christ's life.

THE ROAD TO JERUSALEM

In the scene just before the Transfiguration, Jesus confirmed for the apostles what they all had been suspecting and hoping. He told them that he was indeed Israel's Messiah (see Matthew 16:16–20).

Jesus, however, immediately made it clear that his mission as the Messiah-King would not take him to a luxurious royal palace or a triumphant military victory. Rather, his messianic mission would lead him to the cross: "From that time Jesus began to show his disciples that he must go to Jerusalem and suffer many things from the elders and chief priests and scribes, and be killed, and on the third day be raised" (Matthew 16:21).

Understandably, this message did not go over well with the apostles. How could Israel's Messiah-King suffer such a horrible death? Even Peter was in shock, saying, "God forbid, Lord! This shall never happen to you" (Matthew 16:22).

Now, six days later, Jesus embarks on his final journey to Jerusalem. And his first step on the way is significant. He takes Peter, James, and John up a mountain to prepare them for the difficult road ahead. Jesus knows that when they arrive in Jerusalem, their faith will be tested as never before. They will see their master arrested, beaten, humiliated, stripped, and nailed to a cross. Before they face that trial of faith, Jesus gives them the opportunity to see him in his glory, so that when they see him in his utter humiliation, they might remember that he is the Messiah, the glorified Son of God.

The Byzantine Catholic liturgy expresses this point in a prayer for the Feast of the Transfiguration:

> You were transfigured on the mountain, and your disciples, as much as they were capable of it, beheld your glory, O Christ our God, so that when they should see you crucified they would understand that your Passion was voluntary, and proclaim to the world that you truly are the splendor of the Father.[6]

A New Moses

"And after six days Jesus took with him Peter and James and John his brother, and led them up a high mountain apart. And he was transfigured before them, and his face shone like the sun.... And behold, there appeared to them Moses and Elijah, talking with him.... He was still speaking, when lo, a bright cloud overshadowed them, and a voice from the cloud said, 'This is my beloved Son, with whom I am well pleased; listen to him.' When the disciples heard this, they fell on their faces, and were filled with awe" (Matthew 17:1–3, 5–6).

Accompanying Jesus up the mountain, Peter, James, and John see their master in a completely new light. And what they experience on this high mountain will remind them of what happened to Moses at another famous mountain, Mount Sinai, during another turning point in the history of salvation.

In a key moment from the Exodus story, the Israelites set up camp at Mount Sinai, and there, God established the old covenant, sealing the people as his chosen people. Moses led three of his closest associates—Aaron, Nadab, and Abihu—up the mountain, and the glory of the Lord covered them in the form of a cloud for six days. On the seventh day, a voice called out from the cloud, summoning Moses to receive the Ten Commandments on tablets of stone (see Exodus 24:9–17).

During their stay at Sinai, Moses's face shone brightly whenever he had been talking with God in the sanctuary. When the people saw his radiant face, they were in awe and were afraid to come near him (see Exodus 34:29–30).

In similar fashion, Jesus is about to establish the new covenant, and he goes up a high mountain. Like Moses, Jesus brings with him three of his closest coworkers—Peter, James, and John. While atop the mountain, Christ's face shines brightly, and the three apostles fall down full of awe, reminiscent of the Israelites' reaction to Moses's radiant face.

At the height of the Transfiguration scene, God's glory cloud comes down on the mountain and overshadows them, as it covered Moses and the Israelite leaders on Sinai. And just as a heavenly voice called out from the cloud to give Moses the old law on the tablets of stone, so now the Father's voice calls out from the cloud to reveal the new law in the person of Jesus: "This is my beloved Son, with whom I am well pleased; listen to him" (Matthew 17:5).

The Glorified Face of Christ

Despite the similarities between these two scenes, Matthew is careful to note how Jesus clearly outshines Moses. The new covenant is greater than the old. Moses's face was simply described as shining; Jesus's face is described as shining brightly "like the sun." And he radiates the divine glory so much that even his garments appear as "white as light" (Matthew 17:2).

Moreover, while this event may reveal the glory of Christ's divinity, it also manifests his glorified humanity. Having a shining face does not necessarily mean one is divine. Moses's shining face on Mount Sinai simply showed that he *reflected* the glory of God. Thus, when we contemplate the transfigured Jesus, we see not only a glimpse of his divinity but also a view of his glorified humanity, which perfectly reflects God's glory.

In turn, we also see a snapshot of how our own fallen humanity is meant to be healed, perfected, and clothed with the glory of God—a theme found in St. Paul's Second Letter to the Corinthians. Paul views the transfiguration of Moses's face (and in the background, the transfiguration of Christ's face) as a sign of the transformation God wants to bring about in all our lives: "And we all, with unveiled face, beholding the glory of the Lord, are being changed into his likeness from one degree of

> "Jesus gives them the opportunity to see him in his glory, so that when they see him in his utter humiliation, they might remember he is the Messiah."

glory to another; for this comes from the Lord who is the Spirit" (2 Corinthians 3:18). Indeed, through Christ's transforming grace, we are called to live in a way that reflects the glory of God here on earth. Jesus calls us to be *changed into his likeness from one degree of glory to another.*

The Suffering Servant

"This is my beloved Son, with whom I am well pleased; listen to him" (Matthew 17:5).

Coming just six days after Jesus told the apostles about his upcoming death in Jerusalem, these words from the Father will help assure them that Jesus really is the Messiah and the Son of God. At the same time, these words show the stark reality of Christ's mission to suffer for our sins, for they bring to mind the suffering servant figure from the prophet Isaiah.

As we saw in our consideration of the similar words spoken by the Father at Christ's baptism, Isaiah foretold that God would send an anointed servant to restore Israel and bring salvation to all the nations. God would rejoice in this faithful one, saying, "Behold my servant, whom I uphold, my chosen, in whom my soul delights" (Isaiah 42:1). This servant too would be "wounded for our transgressions" and "bruised for our iniquities" (Isaiah 53:5). Like a lamb led to the slaughter, the Lord's servant would make himself "an offering for sin" (Isaiah 53:7, 10).

Thus, while the Transfiguration exalts Christ and shows forth his glory, the scene again foreshadows Christ's destiny as the suffering servant who will die in Jerusalem for the sins of all humanity. Ultimately, these two themes of Christ's glory and his suffering are meant to go together, for God's glory will be revealed most fully not in worldly splendor or self-exaltation but in his self-giving love for us on the cross. And these themes of the Transfiguration stand as a reminder to us: We are called to radiate God's glory most splendidly through our own sacrificial love here on earth.

....

The Fifth Luminous Mystery
The Institution of the Eucharist
LUKE 22:14–23

I have earnestly desired to eat this passover with you before I suffer; for I tell you I shall not eat it until it is fulfilled in the kingdom of God. (Luke 22:15–16)

The annual Passover ritual was the principal festival for the Jews because it celebrated one of the most important moments in Israel's history: the first Passover in Egypt. On that night, God instructed the enslaved Israelite people to sacrifice a lamb, eat it, and put its blood on their doorposts. It was their last supper in Egypt, for on that night, the Israelites escaped from bondage, and the angel of death struck down all the Egyptian firstborn sons. Every year thereafter, the Jews retold and reenacted the Passover story in their homes and at the temple, to celebrate God's great act of liberation in the Exodus.

BACK TO THE FUTURE

What is important for us to note is that the Jews celebrated the Passover feast as a *memorial*. For the ancient Jews, a liturgical memorial did much more than simply recall a past event. It made that past event present. As a memorial, this annual meal celebration was believed to make the first Passover in Egypt mystically present to those celebrating the ritual.

This is why Jews in Jesus's day believed that when they celebrated the Passover meal, the events surrounding that first Passover in Egypt were brought before them, so that they could be at one with their ancestors and participate in that foundational moment of their nation's history. In fact, some ancient Jews commented that when they celebrated the Passover meal each year, it was as if they themselves were walking out of Egypt with their ancestors in the Exodus.

The Passover not only made the past mystically present but also looked to the future. In Jesus's day, the Passover feast was charged with messianic expectations. There was hope that on some Passover night in the future, God would send the Messiah to the city of Jerusalem to liberate the people. On that much-anticipated night, God would rescue the Jews from their present-day oppressors, just as he freed them from the Egyptians on the night of the first Passover.

With this background in mind, imagine the apostles' great excitement when Jesus gathers them in Jerusalem to celebrate the Passover. Earlier that week, Jesus entered the royal city of Jerusalem and was hailed as a king. Now he tells them it is time to celebrate the Passover. Given the messianic hopes being pinned on Jesus that week and the messianic expectations associated with the Passover each year, this clearly is not going to be any ordinary Passover celebration for the apostles. If Jesus is the Messiah and he has been received as a king in Jerusalem, his calling the apostles together for the freedom meal of the Passover can only signal one thing: The Passover of Passovers is finally here!

The new exodus is about to begin in the Upper Room tonight. Christ's entire public ministry reaches its culmination in this Last Supper. No wonder he says, "I have earnestly desired to eat this passover with you" (Luke 22:15).

Where Is the Lamb?

What is most odd about the Gospel accounts of the Last Supper is that none of them mention the most important part of the Passover meal: the lamb. Not only was the lamb the main course, but it also served as the primary reminder of how the Passover lambs were sacrificed in Egypt so that the Israelite firstborn sons would not be killed in the tenth plague. Yet the Gospel accounts of the Last Supper focus on another type of sacrifice taking place:

> "There was hope that on some Passover night in the future, God would send the Messiah to the city of Jerusalem to liberate the people."

> And he took bread, and when he had given thanks he broke it and gave it to them, saying, "This is my body which is given for you. Do this in remembrance of me." And likewise the cup after supper, saying, "This cup which is poured out for you is the new covenant in my blood." (Luke 22:19–20)

Here Jesus speaks about a body being "given" and blood being "poured out." Every Jew there would recognize that this is sacrificial language taken from the rituals in the temple, where the bodies of the animals are "offered up" and their blood "poured out" over the altar. At this particular Passover meal, however, the body being offered is not that of a lamb or any other animal. Instead, Jesus speaks of his own body being sacrificed and his own blood being poured out.

In other words, Jesus identifies himself with the Passover lamb. Just as the Passover lamb was sacrificed in Egypt to spare the firstborn sons of Israel, so now Jesus is about to be sacrificed on the cross to spare all humanity.

THE LAST SUPPER AND THE CROSS

In this sense, Christ's sacrifice on the cross begins with his institution of the Eucharist at the Last Supper. There in the Upper Room, Jesus voluntarily offers up his body and blood as the Passover Lamb. All that is left is for that sacrifice to be carried out externally in his body on Calvary.

Therefore, when Jesus institutes the Eucharist and says, "Do this in remembrance [as a memorial] of me," he is speaking of his sacrificial self-offering. In the Jewish sense of *memorial*, Jesus is commanding the apostles to *make present* the sacrifice of his body and blood, his total gift of love, which he offers at the Last Supper and carries out on Calvary. The Eucharist is the new Passover of the new covenant.

This is why Catholics speak of the Mass as a sacrifice. It is not a new sacrifice but makes present the one sacrifice of Christ: "When the Church celebrates the Eucharist, she commemorates Christ's Passover, and it is made present: the sacrifice Christ offered once for all on the cross remains ever present" (*CCC*, 1364).

As a biblical memorial, the Passover ritual enabled the Jews to participate in the founding event of their nationhood, the Exodus, which was made present to them in the annual celebration of this feast. Similarly, as the principal memorial of the new covenant, the Eucharist allows us to share in the founding event of Christianity, Jesus's offering of himself on the cross.

Consequently, the *Catechism* teaches that in the Mass, we offer in prayer our entire lives in union with Christ's offering to the Father:

In the Eucharist the sacrifice of Christ becomes also the sacrifice of the members of his Body. The lives of the faithful, their praise, sufferings, prayer, and work are united with those of Christ and with his total offering.... Christ's sacrifice present on the altar makes it possible for all generations of Christians to be united with his offering. (*CCC*, 1368)

The Real Presence

Finally, at the Last Supper, Jesus gives us his very Body and Blood in the Eucharist under the appearances of bread and wine. For the ancient Jews, *the body* expressed the person's soul, and *the blood* was believed to contain the person's life. From this perspective, we can see that in the Eucharist, Jesus intends to give himself completely to us in this sacrament of love.

By giving us his Body and Blood, Christ forges the most profound union we can have with him here on earth. Indeed, reception of the Eucharist is called "Holy Communion," for it is communion with Jesus himself—his Body, Blood, soul, and divinity. As the true "Bread of Life," Jesus himself tells us that the Eucharist is vital for our union with him:

He who eats my flesh and drinks my blood has eternal life, and I will raise him up at the last day. For my flesh is food indeed, and my blood is drink indeed. He who eats my flesh and drinks my blood abides in me, and I in him. As the living Father sent me, and I live because of the Father, so he who eats me will live because of me. (John 6:54–57)

Group Study Questions

1. Why did Jesus, the sinless Savior, ask to be baptized? What light does his baptism shed on his identity and mission?
2. What virtues of Mary are evident from her actions at Cana? How can

you grow in valuing these virtues, developing them in yourself, and encouraging others to pursue them?

3. What was Christ's purpose in the Transfiguration? Why do you think he chose these particular apostles—Peter, James, and John—as witnesses of his revelation (see *CCC*, 554–556, 568)?

4. What insights do Isaiah's Servant Songs (Isaiah 42:1–9; 49:1–13; 50:4–11; 52:13—53:12) bring to your understanding of the Transfiguration?

5. How does the institution of the Eucharist, the final luminous mystery, prepare us to enter into the Sorrowful Mysteries?

CHAPTER TEN

Seeds for Contemplation: Biblical Reflections on the Sorrowful Mysteries

Love and sorrow. In our world today, love is often associated with something joyful, thrilling, and attractive, not something sorrowful. Yet, John Paul II said, "the culmination of the revelation of God's love" can be found precisely in these mysteries that are called 'Sorrowful'" (*RVM*, 22). How might this be?

Beginning with the agony in the garden, Jesus confronts all the temptations and sins of humanity and says to the Father, "Not as I will, but as you will" (Matthew 26:39). Indeed, Christ's "yes" in the Garden of Gethsemane reverses the "no" of Adam in the Garden of Eden.

Yet Christ's love and fidelity come at a price. Jesus firmly resolves to do the Father's will in the first sorrowful mystery, but this will lead him to the scourging at the pillar, the crowning with thorns, the carrying of the cross, and the crucifixion (*RVM*, 22). This is why, when discussing the Sorrowful Mysteries, John Paul II gives most of his attention to the agony in the garden. He says the other four sorrowful mysteries are the result of the first. They highlight how Christ's loving commitment to the Father's will entails great suffering and sacrifice for the sake of our salvation (*RVM*, 22).

In addition to showing God's love for us, these Sorrowful Mysteries unveil the meaning of man himself. Christ's self-giving love in his passion and death serves as the model for understanding the vocation of *all* human beings. We will only find fulfillment by making ourselves a sincere gift to others, as Jesus did for us on Calvary. Indeed, true love and faithfulness ultimately lead to the cross.

....

The First Sorrowful Mystery
The Agony in the Garden
MATTHEW 26:36–46; LUKE 22:39–46

Jesus…went forth with his disciples across the Kidron valley, where there was a garden, which he and his disciples entered. (John 18:1)

The devil's assault against Jesus reaches a new peak here in the Garden of Gethsemane. This is not the first time these two have dueled. Before the start of Christ's public ministry, the devil put Jesus to the test three times in the desert. Jesus resisted each of the devil's temptations, and the angels came to minister to him.

While Jesus could claim an initial victory in that battle in the desert, the war was far from over. As Luke's Gospel ominously notes, "When the devil had ended every temptation, he departed from him until an opportune time" (Luke 4:13). In other words, the devil was waiting for the right time to come back and put Jesus to the test again.

That "opportune time" of the devil has arrived in the Garden of Gethsemane, in this first sorrowful mystery. Although Jesus engaged in several skirmishes with demons throughout his proclamation of the kingdom, on this night, he faces a frontal assault with the devil. In the events surrounding this scene, Luke's Gospel highlights how Satan is mounting his final attack: The devil has just entered Judas (see Luke 22:3–4), Satan seeks to have all the disciples be sifted like wheat (Luke 22:31), and Jesus describes his arrest as "the power of darkness" coming upon him (Luke 22:53). Luke makes this point clear: The final battle is about to begin.

LEAD US NOT INTO TEMPTATION

As Jesus enters the garden with his disciples, he tells them, "Pray that you may not enter into temptation" (Luke 22:40). The word in New Testament Greek for "temptation" is *peirasmos*, which is the same word used to describe the temptations that Satan inflicted on Christ in the desert. With this exhortation in the garden, Jesus signals that the hour of the devil's most severe testing is here. Just as he did not give in to the devil's testing in the desert, Jesus encourages the disciples to resist the testing that they are about to face as they witness their master being arrested, condemned, scourged, and crucified.

These words of Jesus also echo the last lines of the Lord's Prayer, which he taught the disciples earlier in his public ministry: "And lead us not into temptation [*peirasmos*]" (Matthew 6:13; see Luke 11:4). While God may allow people to be tested in order to strengthen their faith, Jesus asks his disciples to pray that they not "enter into" those tests, in the sense of giving in to them. In other words, they are to pray that they may not yield to the trials that they are about to endure (see *CCC*, 2846).

SORROWFUL UNTO DEATH

Jesus then invites three of his apostles—Peter, James, and John—to come with him as he begins to pray on his own (see Matthew 26:37). These are the same three who witnessed Christ's face shining brightly with God's glory at the Transfiguration. Now they will be near Jesus as the sweat from his face becomes like drops of blood in this moment of great agony (Luke 22:44).

Troubled and afflicted, Jesus says to these three close friends, "My soul is very sorrowful, even to death; remain here, and watch with me" (Matthew 26:38). To be sorrowful unto death means to be pushed to the extreme limits with grief. The words describe almost unendurable suffering. Spoken in the context of Judas's betrayal and Christ's imminent arrest, Jesus's sorrow echoes the words of Sirach 37:2: "Is it not a grief to the death when a companion and friend turns to enmity?"

Knowing all that is about to happen to him, Jesus kneels down and falls on his face—highlighting his distress and the intensity of the prayer that follows: "Father, if it be possible, let this cup pass from me; nevertheless, not as I will, but as you will" (Matthew 26:39; see Luke 22:42).

At first glance, this is a perplexing prayer. What does it mean? Is Jesus, at the last moment, trying to back out of his mission to redeem the world? Is he trying to persuade the Father to find another option so he can avoid drinking the cup of suffering on Calvary?

"Jesus signals that the hour of the devil's most severe testing is here."

PASS THE CUP?

"If possible, let this cup pass from me." This prayer simply reflects the fact that Jesus is truly a man. Suffering and death are repulsive to human nature. If Jesus is truly human, the suffering that he is about to endure on the cross would not be perceived as something pleasant. As the *Catechism* explains, Christ's prayer in Gethsemane "expresses the horror that death represented for his human nature" (*CCC*, 612).

At the same time, unlike our weak wills wounded by sin, Jesus's human will is perfectly united to the Father's (see *CCC*, 475). Thus, he immediately says, "Not as I will, but as you will." In other words, while Christ feels a full aversion to death, he also is completely willing to embrace that suffering on the cross for the sake of his Father's plan of salvation.

In the face of suffering, fallen humanity often hesitates to do the right thing. We may shrink altogether from doing God's will. Too often we are afraid to make sacrifices, and we let our fear of suffering keep us from doing what is right. Jesus, however, faces that suffering, feels the full force of it, and freely embraces it for the sake of our salvation, in full acceptance of his Father's will.

The Agony

And there appeared to him an angel from heaven, strengthening him. And being in an agony he prayed more earnestly; and his sweat became like great drops of blood falling down upon the ground. (Luke 22:43–44)

In response to Jesus's prayer, the Father sends an angel to strengthen him for his passion and death. Just as the angels ministered to him during his first battle with Satan in the desert (see Matthew 4:11), so now an angel of the Lord comes to his aid as the devil's final onslaught begins. The description of Jesus's sweat becoming like drops of blood shows the intensity of his ordeal. The turmoil in Jesus's soul is manifested through his body.

Some scholars have suggested that Luke's description of Jesus being in "agony" recalls the ordeal ancient runners faced as they were about to begin a race. As they approached the starting line, the runners sometimes would become so intense that sweat would break out all over their bodies. This moment was known as the runner's "agony."[1]

In the Garden of Gethsemane, Jesus faces a much more serious contest, a battle with the devil for the salvation of the world. Poised at the starting line of this redemptive contest, Jesus, like a runner, sweats profusely, manifesting the intensity of the ordeal he is about to undergo.

Back to Paradise

Finally, in this scene we can see Jesus reliving the test of Adam and proving himself to be a faithful Son of God precisely where Adam was unfaithful. For example, the devil tested Adam in the Garden of Eden, and he tested Jesus in the Garden of Gethsemane. Adam did not trust the Father in his time of testing, preferring his own will to God's, whereas Jesus says to the Father, "Not as I will, but as you will." Adam's disobedience led him to the forbidden Tree of Knowledge of Good and Evil, while Christ's prayer of obedience leads him to the wood of the cross—which Christians later will call the new Tree of Life.

As the new Adam, Jesus takes on the effects of Adam's sin. Consider how, as a result of the first sin, Adam became ashamed in his *nakedness*, was expelled from *Paradise*, and received a number of curses. God said to Adam,

> Cursed is the ground because of you; in toil you shall eat of it all the days of your life; thorns and thistles it shall bring forth to you.... In the sweat of your face you shall eat bread till you return to the ground, for out of it you were taken; you are dust, and to dust you shall return. (Genesis 3:17–19)

Adam's labor would no longer be easy. Cast out of the *garden*, now he had to toil in *sweat*, and the ground would often produce *thorns* and thistles instead of fruit. The greatest curse of all was *death*. Adam no longer would live forever but would return to the *ground* at the end of his life.

Taking on the curses of Adam, Jesus *sweats* intensely in Gethsemane as he clings to his Father's will. On Good Friday, he is crowned with *thorns*, stripped *naked*, and nailed to a cross. He suffers *death* and is buried in the *ground*, in a *garden* near Calvary (see John 19:41).

Yet, while dying on the cross, Jesus announces that he is returning to *Paradise*, and he will take the sons of Adam with him. One of the first to enter his kingdom is the "good thief," to whom Jesus says, "Today you will be with me in Paradise" (Luke 23:43).

As the new Adam, Jesus is faithful where the first Adam was unfaithful. He takes on the curses that have plagued the human family since the Fall. In his passion and death, Christ thus undoes the first sin and restores the sons of Adam to the Father.

The Second Sorrowful Mystery
The Scourging at the Pillar
MATTHEW 27:15–26

He was wounded for our transgressions, he was bruised for our iniquities. (Isaiah 53:5)

In matters of legal discipline, the Jews showed at least some restraint in their use of the whip. In order to ensure that whippings would not get out of hand, a criminal could be given no more than forty lashes (see Deuteronomy 25:3). The Pharisees, worried that some enthusiastic executioners might accidentally cross that legal limit, set the maximum number of lashes at thirty-nine.

> "Christians all over the world continue to recall the tragic result of Pilate's lack of courage: 'He suffered under Pontius Pilate.'"

Roman scourging was not nearly as merciful. The practice was much more severe than a whipping, and there were no limits. A Roman scourging normally involved the prisoner's being stripped and tied to a pillar or a low post. The whip had leather thongs ending with sharp pieces of bone or metal spikes, which would rip a person's flesh in a single stroke. If used repeatedly on a criminal's back, these instruments could cut into the muscle and expose the person's bones. Scourgings sometimes caused death.

A Roman scourging was not simply another form of punishment. Sometimes the Romans used it to torture prisoners in order to extract information from them. Other times, scourging served as a prelude to crucifixion, to inflict intense physical trauma before the prisoner carried his cross. In this latter case, scourging not only increased the suffering of the prisoner but also allowed the Roman soldiers some control over how long the prisoner would survive. A long, severe beating would greatly weaken the prisoner and result in a quicker death on the cross.

This latter type of scourging is what Jesus goes through on Good

Friday. It is his first step toward the cross, by which he will redeem the world.

THE BARABBAS CHOICE

What leads to Jesus's being scourged at the pillar?

After being arrested and put on trial, Jesus is condemned to death by the Jewish leaders in Jerusalem. However, since they are under Roman law, they cannot carry out capital punishment on their own. Only the Roman government has the authority to execute. That is why the chief priests hand Jesus over to Pontius Pilate, the Roman governor ruling Judea. They charge that Jesus is a revolutionary who stirs up the people, and they want Pilate to have him executed (see Luke 23:2, 5).

Pilate, however, is used to dealing with rebels, and he realizes that Jesus is no serious threat to the Roman Empire. Pilate understands that what lies at the heart of the chief priests' contention against this innocent man is a religious rivalry: "He knew it was out of envy that they had delivered him up" (Matthew 27:18).

Since Pilate has a custom of freeing one Jewish prisoner during Passover, he offers to release Jesus. However, the chief priests and the crowds they incite ask for the release of another man, Barabbas, a notorious insurrectionist. This is not simply a choice between a revolutionary criminal and an innocent man. There is much symbolism in this choice, for the name *Barabbas* literally means "son of the father." In choosing Barabbas, the crowds favor this false "son of the father," who as a Jewish rebel represents violence and vengeance. They reject Jesus, the true Son of the Father, who represents peace and forgiveness.

"Pilate said to them, 'Then what shall I do with Jesus who is called Christ?' They all said, 'Let him be crucified.' And he said, 'Why, what evil has he done?' But they shouted all the more, 'Let him be crucified'" (Matthew 27:22–23).

PILATE'S CONSCIENCE

So when Pilate saw that he was gaining nothing, but rather that a riot was beginning, he took water and washed his hands before the crowd, saying, 'I am innocent of this righteous man's blood; see to it yourselves.' And all the people answered, 'His blood be on us and on our children!' Then he released for them Barabbas, and having scourged Jesus, delivered him to be crucified. (Matthew 27:24–26)

The opposition is too strong. Pilate realizes that he cannot convince the crowd and that their hostility is mounting to a riot. Rather than take a stand to protect the innocent Jesus, Pilate cowardly caves in to the pressure and allows Jesus to be scourged and crucified. In an effort to quell his troubled conscience, Pilate washes his hands in a symbolic gesture, hoping to distance himself from responsibility for Christ's death.

History, however, will not let Pilate get away with that. He will be immortalized in the Creed as the Roman ruler who allowed Jesus to be killed. To this very day, Christians all over the world continue to recall the tragic result of Pilate's lack of courage: "[Jesus] suffered under Pontius Pilate, was crucified, died, and was buried."

We too will face choices about whether to stand up for what is true, good, and just or to cowardly go with the pressures of the crowd, the secular culture, or what's popular. Will we stand with Jesus and defend marriage, protect human life at all stages, and accept our responsibility to care for the poor? Or will we say with Pilate, "What is truth?" and go along with the mainstream, relativistic ways of thinking and living today? As with Pilate, our choices will be revealed—probably not in a creedal statement of the Church and maybe not in our lifetime, but at the very least, on the last day at the final judgment.

....

The Third Sorrowful Mystery

The Crowning with Thorns

MATTHEW 27:27–29

Plaiting a crown of thorns they put it on his head, and put a reed in his right hand. And kneeling before him they mocked him, saying, "Hail, King of the Jews." (Matthew 27:29)

Imagine hundreds of Roman soldiers kneeling before a man who is crowned, clothed in a royal cloak, and holding a scepter in his right hand. They all fall down before him and give him homage, saying, "Hail, the King!"

In most contexts, such a display would demonstrate a king's royal splendor. In the third sorrowful mystery, however, this scene represents the height of humiliation as the Roman soldiers scoff at Jesus and ridicule his claim to be the king of the Jews.

> "Despite their cruel intentions, the soldiers unwittingly proclaim the truth of Jesus Christ: He is the true King of the Jews."

HAIL TO THE KING

Then the soldiers of the governor took Jesus into the praetorium, and they gathered the whole battalion before him. And they stripped him and put a scarlet robe upon him, and plaiting a crown of thorns they put it on his head, and put a reed in his right hand. And kneeling before him they mocked him, saying, 'Hail, King of the Jews!'" (Matthew 27:27–29)

The praetorium was the official residence of Pilate, the Roman governor. After being scourged, Jesus is taken there as a final stop on the way to his crucifixion. Matthew notes that "a whole battalion," which is a cohort of up to six hundred soldiers, meets him there to make sport of his claim to be Israel's Messiah.

The soldiers begin by dressing Jesus like a king. For royal garments, they put a scarlet robe around him—scarlet being the color worn by Roman military, by high-ranking officials, and by the emperor himself.[2] For a diadem, they weave a crown of thorns together and place it on his head. For a scepter, they place a reed in his right hand, symbolizing a king's authority.

This costume that the soldiers force on Jesus is cruel sarcasm. They proceed to kneel before him and act as if they are paying him homage. They even mimic the royal address one would give to the emperor— "Hail, Caesar!"—by saying to the scourged, condemned, and humiliated Jesus, "Hail, King of the Jews!"

This scene challenges us to consider more carefully how we use our words. Do we use our speech to build up? To honor, thank, and praise others? To talk about the things that matter most in life: friendship, family, and whatever is true and good and beautiful? Or do we use our words as the Roman soldiers did, to tear down: to criticize, gossip, ridicule, or condemn? Do we use our words to talk about base things, never rising above the trivial, things that do not build up the body of Christ?

THE IRONY OF THE CROWN

Christians will see a great irony in this scene. While the soldiers scoff at Jesus, they have no idea how appropriate their words actually are. Despite their cruel intentions, they unwittingly proclaim the truth of Jesus Christ: He really is the Messiah, the true King of the Jews. The homage these pagan soldiers pay in jest anticipates the sincere honor countless Christians will give Jesus as they worship him as their Lord and King.

Most ironically, the soldiers who in their mockery kneel before Jesus will find themselves in the same position of reverence at the Last Judgment, when the words of St. Paul will be fulfilled: "That at the name of Jesus *every knee should bow*, in heaven and on earth and under the earth, and every tongue confess that Jesus Christ is Lord, to the glory of God the Father" (Philippians 2:10–11).

But now the soldiers' mockery turns to physical abuse. The immature battalion begins to spit at Jesus, slap him on the face, and strike his head with a rod (see Matthew 27:30; John 19:3). Just as the chief priests mocked Jesus, slapped him, and spat in his face during his trial before the Sanhedrin, so now the Romans taunt Jesus and afflict him with similar forms of violence. One might hear echoes of Isaiah's prophecy about the suffering servant of the Lord: "I gave my back to the those who struck me, and my cheeks to those who pulled out the beard [that is, those who insulted me]; I hid not my face from shame and spitting" (Isaiah 50:6).

THE KING'S ENTHRONEMENT

This is not the only scene from Christ's passion that carries royal overtones. During the trial, Pilate asks Jesus, "Are you the King of the Jews?" (Matthew 27:11). Pilate later presents Jesus to the crowds, saying, "Here is your King!" When the people request that Jesus be crucified, Pilate asks them, "Shall I crucify your King?" (John 19:14–15).

At the crucifixion, Pilate orders a sign to be placed over Christ's cross: "This is Jesus the King of the Jews" (Matthew 27:37). While on the cross, Jesus hears the mocking of the chief priests, scribes, and elders: "He is the King of Israel; let him come down now from the cross, and we will believe in him" (Matthew 27:42). And shortly before Jesus dies, the "good thief" crucified alongside him says, "Jesus, remember me when you come in your kingly power" (Luke 23:42).

Thus, when the ridiculing soldiers crown Jesus with thorns, dress him in royal colors, kneel before him, and mockingly say, "Hail, King of the Jews!" this is just one of many instances of the kingship theme surrounding Christ's passion and death. From a human perspective, this seems to be an odd time to highlight Christ's royal majesty. How could Jesus be a triumphant king when he is stripped, scourged, beaten, mocked, and nailed to a cross? Christ's death seems like a humiliating defeat, not a royal triumph!

Yet, by stressing Christ's kingship precisely in his passion and death, the Gospels boldly proclaim the mystery of the cross. The cross is not a sign of defeat. Rather, it is the greatest victory the world has ever known. It is on Calvary that Jesus establishes his kingdom by conquering sin and death. In this sense, the crucifixion really is Christ's enthronement as King. Through his passion, death, and resurrection, Jesus defeats the devil and invites us to enter into the kingdom of God, sharing in his reign over sin and death.

> "Like Simon, we might not seek out these crosses, but do we embrace them?"

The Fourth Sorrowful Mystery
The Carrying of the Cross
LUKE 23:26–31

And they led him out to crucify him. (Mark 15:20)

Roman crucifixions generally took place outside the city walls along crowded roads so that many people could witness what happened when someone revolted against Rome. At the crucifixion site, the vertical part of the cross was planted in the ground. The condemned criminal was given the crossbeam in the city and had it placed over his shoulders like a yoke, with his arms hooked over it. He would be forced to carry the crossbeam through the streets and out the city gates.

It would be highly unusual for the Romans to permit another person to carry the crossbeam for a criminal condemned to crucifixion. Yet that is exactly what happens with Jesus in this fourth sorrowful mystery.

Simon of Cyrene

"And as they led him away, they seized one Simon of Cyrene, who was coming in from the country, and laid on him the cross, to carry it behind Jesus" (Luke 23:26).

Who is this Simon of Cyrene? And why is he forced to carry Christ's cross?

The fact that the Romans break from the normal practice of having the criminal carry his own cross indicates just how beaten Jesus must be from his scourging. He is so physically weak that the soldiers fear he may not make it to the execution site outside the city. Roman soldiers had authority to require assistance from civilians, and they press into service Simon of Cyrene.

We do not know much about this Simon. The Gospels tell us he was from the city of Cyrene, which was a center of Jewish population in northern Africa. He may have been in Jerusalem as a pilgrim for the Passover feast. It is also possible that Simon was a settler in the city, since devout Jews from Cyrene stayed in Jerusalem, and there was a synagogue for Cyrenians there (see Acts 6:9).

Luke's Gospel notes that Simon is "coming in from the country" when he is enlisted to carry Jesus's cross. He probably has no idea about the dramatic events occurring in Jerusalem that day. The fact that he was not in Jerusalem during the uproar surrounding Christ's trial and condemnation tells us that he did not participate in the mob shouting for Jesus's execution. Not all of the Jews are intensely opposed to Jesus.

On entering the city gates, Simon would hear the riotous crowd coming toward him down a narrow Jerusalem street. Some are wailing in mourning, while others probably are shouting insults. He would see Roman soldiers pushing a staggering man, who is barely able to carry a crossbeam. Finding himself engulfed in this tumultuous procession to a crucifixion, Simon is suddenly singled out by the Roman soldiers. They take the crossbeam off of the condemned man, put it on Simon's shoulders, and force him to carry it.

Luke notes that Simon carries the cross *behind* Jesus. This is symbolic of Christ's teaching about discipleship: "If any man would come after me, let him deny himself and take up his cross daily and follow me" (Luke 9:23). While it is true that Simon carries Christ's cross by compulsion, a tradition arose that this encounter with the cross of Jesus transformed him and that he and his family eventually became Christian. Some point to a verse in Mark's Gospel to support this tradition.

Mark's account of this scene mentions that Simon has two sons, Alexander and Rufus (see Mark 15:21). This Rufus might be the well-known Rufus in the Roman Church, whom Paul later calls "eminent in the Lord" (Romans 16:13)—indeed, the only other Rufus mentioned in the New Testament.

How do we respond to unexpected crosses that come our way—whether the little troubles we meet each day or the bigger trials that come in life? Like Simon, we might not seek out these crosses, but do we embrace them? Do we trust that God can bring some good out of them for us, just as he brings good for Simon of Cyrene?

From Majesty to Mourning

And there followed him a great multitude of the people, and of women who bewailed and lamented him. (Luke 23:27)

Ironically, Jesus rode majestically into Jerusalem on a colt earlier that week, with a "whole multitude" of disciples rejoicing and blessing him as "the King who comes in the name of the Lord" (Luke 19:37–38). Now he exits the holy city, humiliated and scourged, with "a great multitude" of people mourning his crucifixion. The weeping and lamenting of the women echo the prophecy of Zechariah 12:10:

And I will pour out on the house of David and the inhabitants of

Jerusalem a spirit of compassion and supplication, so that, when they look on him whom they have pierced, they shall mourn for him, as one mourns for an only child, and weep bitterly over him, as one weeps over a first-born.

Nevertheless, even the compassionate tears of the women may not be enough to prevent the judgment that will come upon this city that is killing the Messiah.

Blessed Are the Barren?

But Jesus turning to them said, "Daughters of Jerusalem, do not weep for me, but weep for yourselves and for your children. For behold, the days are coming when they will say, 'Blessed are the barren, and the wombs that never bore, and the breasts that never gave suck!' Then they will begin to say to the mountains, 'Fall on us'; and to the hills, 'Cover us.' For if they do this when the wood is green, what will happen when it is dry?" (Luke 23:28–31)

What provokes such a harsh beatitude from Jesus—"Blessed are the barren, and the wombs that never bore"? Within the ancient Jewish context, barrenness was a woman's greatest nightmare. Why would Jesus dare to call it a blessing?

Christ is starkly warning the women of what will happen to Jerusalem if the city does not repent. When Jesus foretells how people will ask the mountains and hills to fall on them, he is alluding to Hosea's prophecy of judgment on Samaria: "They shall say to the mountains, Cover us, and to the hills, Fall upon us" (Hosea 10:8). Just as the kingdom of Samaria persisted in its rebellion against God and was destroyed by a foreign army, so will Jerusalem be demolished unless it changes its ways and repents for its leaders who are having Israel's Messiah killed. Christ is warning of the destruction of Jerusalem in AD 70, when Roman armies will devastate the city with war, famine, and fire.

THE DRY WOOD

We can see this even more when Jesus leaves the weeping women with the cryptic remark, "For if they do this when the wood is green, what will happen when it is dry?" (Luke 23:31).

Green wood is moist and not able to be used in a fire, while dry wood burns rather easily. Jesus is saying that he is like green wood—innocent and not deserving of punishment. If Jesus suffers so much under the Romans as an innocent man, imagine the type of suffering the guilty in Jerusalem will face when real revolutionaries rebel against Roman authority.

> "The goal of crucifixion was not simply to execute but to do so with the maximum amount of pain and public humiliation."

Indeed, much of Jerusalem will be burned like dry wood as Roman forces squash the Jewish uprising in the generation after Jesus. There will be such atrocities in Jerusalem's fiery destruction that Jesus can speak of women wishing they were barren instead of having to see their children suffer. That is why Jesus says, "Do not weep for me, but weep for yourselves and for your children." As one commentator put it, "The youngsters playing in the streets in Jesus's day would become the firebrands of the next generation, and would suffer the terrible consequences [of the Roman armies]. The mothers should save their tears for when they would really be needed."[3]

The Fifth Sorrowful Mystery
The Crucifixion
MATTHEW 27:35–66; MARK 15:25–47; LUKE 23:33–56;
JOHN 19:18–42

And it was the third hour, when they crucified him. And the inscription of the charge against him read, "The King of the Jews." And with him they crucified two robbers, one on his right and one on his left. And those who passed by derided him, wagging their heads, and saying, "Aha! You who would destroy the temple and build it in three days, save yourself, and come down from the cross!" So also the chief priests mocked him to one another with the scribes, saying, "He saved others; he cannot save himself. Let the Christ, the King of Israel, come down now from the cross, that we may see and believe." Those who were crucified with him also reviled him. (Mark 15:25–32)

The Romans used crucifixion as punishment for the most serious of crimes, especially that of revolting against Roman rule. This form of punishment was so abhorrent that the ancient Roman orator Cicero once said that the mere mention of the word *cross* "should be far removed not only from the person of a Roman citizen but from his thoughts, his eyes, and his ears."[4]

The goal of crucifixion was not simply to execute but to do so with the maximum amount of pain and public humiliation. Men condemned to this type of death were stripped of their clothes and nailed or bound to a cross with their arms extended and raised. Thus immobilized, their exposed bodies had no means of coping with heat, cold, insects, or pain.

Since crucifixion did not damage any vital organ or cause excessive bleeding, death came slowly, sometimes over several days as the weight of the unsupported body gradually caused the breathing muscles to give in. Eventually the crucified man succumbed to shock or asphyxiation.

Sometimes a condemned man was given a footrest at the bottom of the vertical beam. This, however, was no act of mercy. It simply enabled the crucified man to lift himself up for a breath and thus survive in agonizing pain for a longer period of time.

Crucifixion sent a powerful message to the Jews: Don't even think about rising up against us. The cross stood as one of the greatest symbols of Jewish suffering under the curse of Roman domination. It is precisely into this suffering that Israel's Messiah enters as he is crucified on Calvary.

"Father, Forgive Them"

And when they came to the place which is called The Skull, there they crucified him, and the criminals, one on the right and one on the left. And Jesus said, "Father, forgive them; for they know not what they do." (Luke 23:33–34)

Although crucifixion is intended to take away every vestige of a criminal's freedom and dignity, the Gospels show us that Jesus is no ill-fated victim. He emerges on the cross as one who is on a mission. He is still in control, trusting in the Father and carrying out his redemptive plan.

First, consider how the cross does not inhibit Christ's ministry of mercy. Indeed, from there he performs the most powerful act of forgiveness one could offer—forgiving one's enemies. Jesus has been falsely accused, wrongly ridiculed, and unjustly tortured. The Jewish leaders have slapped him, the Roman battalion has scourged him, and now the soldiers have crucified him. Yet Jesus responds with mercy. In the midst of his riveting pain on the cross, he shows sympathy and understanding for those who are killing him: "Father, forgive them; for they know not what they do."

Thus, Jesus embodies his teaching to love those who have injured us: "Love your enemies, do good to those who hate you, bless those who curse you, pray for those who abuse you" (Luke 6:27–28). Jesus not only forgives but even makes excuses for his executioners, giving them the benefit of the doubt. He understands that these people would not put him to death if they truly realized what they were doing.

As the *Catechism* explains, we are called to imitate Christ's merciful response to evils committed against us—to turn injuries into intercessory prayer for those who hurt us. "It is not in our power not to feel or to forget an offense; but the heart that offers itself to the Holy Spirit turns injury into compassion and purifies the memory in transforming the hurt into intercession" (*CCC*, 2843).

"You Will Be with Me in Paradise"

One of the criminals who were hanged railed at him, saying, "Are you not the Christ? Save yourself and us!" But the other rebuked him, saying, "Do you not fear God, since you are under the same sentence of condemnation? And we indeed justly; for we are receiving the due reward of our deeds; but this man has done nothing wrong." And he said, "Jesus, remember me when you come in your kingly power." And he said to him, "Truly, I say to you, today you will be with me in Paradise." (Luke 23:39–43)

Here we see a second example of how the nails cannot keep Jesus from carrying out his saving mission. Even while facing his own death on the cross, Jesus grants salvation to the dying, repentant criminal.

After the Jewish leaders and Roman soldiers mock Jesus for claiming to be Israel's Messiah-King (see Luke 23:35–36), one of the criminals with Jesus joins in: "Are you not the Christ? Save yourself and us!" The other crucified man, however, rebukes the first. Humbly, he admits his own guilt and recognizes that Jesus is innocent and undeserving of this cruel punishment. He turns to Jesus and says, "Remember me when you come in your kingly power."

The good thief's words are remarkable. Unlike everyone who is mocking Jesus, this man does not think Christ's death is a defeat but rather anticipates in it the beginning of the kingdom. This criminal thus is the first to recognize that the cursed Roman cross upon which Jesus hangs is actually the means by which Christ's kingdom will be established. He sees that Jesus's crucifixion is somehow his enthronement as king.

Jesus responds to this man's great faith and last-minute conversion by granting him far more than he requested. Jesus does not simply promise to remember him when he enters into his kingdom, but he announces this man's imminent salvation: "Today you will be with me in Paradise" (Luke 23:43).

"Behold, Your Mother"

When Jesus saw his mother, and the disciple whom he loved standing near, he said to his mother, "Woman, behold, your son!" Then he said to the disciple, "Behold, your mother!" And from that hour the disciple took her to his own home. (John 19:26–27)

Standing near the cross, Mary watches her son suffer this most horrible of deaths. She can do nothing to help him or even comfort him. Simeon's words from the Presentation come to fulfillment: "A sword will pierce through your own soul also" (Luke 2:35).

Now, in the last moments of his life, just before he says, "It is finished," Jesus performs one more act of kindness on the cross. He entrusts his mother to "the beloved disciple," John. On a practical level, this act will provide care for Mary after he dies. On another level, however, bringing Mary and the beloved disciple into a mother-son relationship has profound theological meaning. As many Catholics throughout the centuries have seen, Jesus does not just show concern for his mother but actually entrusts all Christians, who are represented by the beloved disciple, to her maternal care.

In John's Gospel, certain individuals represent larger groups. For example, Nicodemus, the Pharisee who meets Jesus at night and does not understand his message, represents the many Pharisees who have difficulty understanding and accepting Christ's mission (see John 3:1–21). The Samaritan woman who meets Jesus at the well and undergoes conversion represents the many Samaritans who will come to believe in Christ (see John 4:1–42). Similarly, "the beloved disciple" in John's Gospel is the apostle John, who also represents all faithful Christians.

"The Beloved Disciple"

In John's Gospel, we see that the beloved disciple is the one who shares a close intimacy with Jesus at the Last Supper (see John 13:23), remains with Jesus during his crucifixion (see John 19:26), is the first to believe in the risen Lord (see John 20:8), and continues to bear testimony to Jesus (see John 21:7, 20, 24). In other words, the beloved disciple is an ideal follower of Christ. As the model disciple in John's Gospel, this individual also represents all faithful Christian disciples.

This is why Catholics have seen in this action at the cross a basis for understanding Mary's spiritual motherhood of all Christians. Since the beloved disciple represents all faithful followers of Christ, Mary, who becomes the mother of the beloved disciple in this scene, becomes also the mother of all the faithful Christians he represents. As John Paul II has commented,

> The Mother of Christ, who stands at the very center of this mystery—a mystery which embraces each individual and all humanity—is given as mother to every single individual and all mankind. The man at the foot of the Cross is John, "the disciple whom he loved." But it is not he alone. Following tradition, the [Second Vatican] Council does not hesitate to call Mary "the Mother of Christ and mother of mankind."… "Indeed she is 'clearly the mother of the members of Christ…since she cooperated out of love so that there might be born in the Church the faithful.'"[5]

"Why Have You Abandoned Me?"

Now from the sixth hour there was darkness over all the land until the ninth hour. And about the ninth hour Jesus cried with a loud voice, "Eli, Eli, lama sabach-thani?" that is, "My God, my God, why have you forsaken me?" (Matthew 27:45–46).

On the cross, Jesus enters into the depths of Israel's sufferings and the pains of all humanity as he takes on the sins of the world. Many have interpreted his words, "My God, my God, why have you forsaken me?" as a cry of despair, signifying his alienation from the Father, who has rejected the Son on Calvary. Yet on closer examination, we see that Jesus is quoting the opening line of Psalm 22, which is not a psalm of despair but a hymn of tremendous hope in times of intense trial.

The psalmist experiences such hardship that he feels *as if* God has abandoned him:

My God, my God, why have you forsaken me?

Why are you so far from helping me, from the words of my groaning?

O my God, I cry by day, but you do not answer;

and by night, but find no rest. (Psalm 22:1–2)

The psalm goes on to describe the righteous man's sufferings in ways that foreshadow Christ's crucifixion. For example:

But I am a worm, and no man;

scorned by men, and despised by the people.

All who see me *mock at me,*

they make mouths at me, *they wag their heads;*

"He committed his cause to the LORD; let him deliver him,

let him rescue him, for he delights in him!" (Psalm 22:6–8, italics added)

These verses anticipate the events on Calvary. People pass by the crucified Christ, "wagging their heads" and scoffing at him, while the Jewish leaders almost repeat the words of the psalm: "He trusts in God; let God deliver him now, if he desires him" (Matthew 27:43).

Psalm 22 also foreshadows the type of physical suffering Christ endures:

They have *pierced my hands and feet—*

I can count all my bones—
  they stare and gloat over me;
they *divide my garments* among them,
  and for my raiment they *cast lots*. (Psalm 22:16–18, italics added)

We see these verses fulfilled on Calvary. The Roman soldiers pierce Jesus by nailing him to the cross, and they divide his garments among them by casting lots (see Matthew 27:35).

CONFIDENCE ON THE CROSS

Yet, however terrible the psalmist's sufferings may be, Psalm 22 expresses the righteous man's great hope in the face of severe trial. In the midst of being persecuted and beaten, and feeling as if God is far away, the psalmist still trusts that the Lord will hear his plea and rescue him. He recalls how the Lord has answered the cry of the righteous throughout history and trusts that God will hear him and come to his aid as well:

Yet you are holy,
  enthroned on the praises of Israel.
In you our fathers trusted;
  they trusted, and you delivered them.
To you they cried, and were saved. (Psalm 22:3–5)

The psalmist then calls on the Lord as his only source of strength:

Be not far from me,
  for trouble is near
  and there is none to help. (Psalm 22:11)

The psalm concludes with a resounding confidence that God will vindicate the psalmist and all those who suffer for righteousness' sake:

I will tell of your name to my brethren;
  in the midst of the congregation I will praise you:
You who fear the LORD, praise him!
  all you sons of Jacob, glorify him,

and stand in awe of him, all you sons of Israel!
For he has not despised or abhorred
   the affliction of the afflicted;
and he has not hid his face from him,
   but has heard, when he cried to him.

From you comes my praise in the great congregation;
   my vows I will pay before those who fear him.
The afflicted shall eat and be satisfied;
   those who seek him shall praise the LORD!
May your hearts live for ever! (Psalm 22:22–26)

This is not the cry of a man in utter despair. It is the voice of a man who entrusts himself to the Lord. He praises the God who hears the cries of the afflicted, and he has firm confidence that the Lord will rescue him. The psalmist even foretells how, in this vindication of the righteous, God's reign will extend to all nations:

All the ends of the earth shall remember
   and turn to the LORD;
and all the families of the nations
   shall worship before him.
For dominion belongs to the Lord,
   and he rules over the nations. (Psalm 22:27–28)

In quoting the first line of Psalm 22—"My God, my God, why have you forsaken me?"—Jesus evokes the whole psalm. Since the psalm expresses trust in God and ends on a clearly victorious note, we should not interpret Christ's words as a cry of despair.

Certainly Jesus expresses his union with us in the depths of our suffering and sin. At the same time, however, his reference to Psalm 22 expresses his total trust that the Father will vindicate him. Thus, Christ's cry on Good Friday anticipates his victory on Easter Sunday, when he will rise from the dead and restore us as sons and daughters of the Father. Indeed, through Christ's resurrection, the high point of Psalm 22 will be fulfilled: God will reign over all the earth, rescuing all who suffer and bringing "all the families of the nations" together to worship before him (Psalm 22:27).

GROUP STUDY QUESTIONS

1. Pope St. John Paul II wrote that Jesus's "abject suffering reveals not only the love of God but also the meaning of man himself" (*RVM*, 22). How can meditating on the Sorrowful Mysteries enlighten your identity and vocation? What does this mystery tell us about the meaning of human life?

2. What did the disciples' sleep add to Jesus's sorrow in Gethsemane? What have you added to Jesus's sorrow?

3. What did the angel from heaven do for Jesus in the garden (see Luke 22:43)? How can you be with Jesus in his suffering and death? What consolations can you offer him?

4. Jesus said to his disciples, "Truly, truly, I say to you, you will weep and lament, but the world will rejoice; you will be sorrowful, but your sorrow will turn into joy" (John 16:20). How can sorrow become joy? What is *the joy of the Gospel*?

5. What irony do you see in the soldiers' mockery of Jesus and crowning him with thorns (see Matthew 27:27–29; Mark 15:16–20; John 19:2–3)?

6. The Sorrowful Mysteries are probably the most difficult for us to contemplate. Why do we ponder these events of the now risen and glorified Christ?

7. Where do we see Mary in the Sorrowful Mysteries? How is her presence significant to you? How is it significant to the Church?

CHAPTER ELEVEN

Seeds for Contemplation:
Biblical Reflections on the Glorious
Mysteries

It's fascinating to see how the five Glorious Mysteries work together. They each draw us deeper into the mystery of Christ's resurrection, with the descent of the Holy Spirit as the hinge and Mary as the preeminent model for what God wants to accomplish in all our lives.

In the first mystery, Jesus rises triumphant over sin, death, and all that keeps us from union with God. Then in the second mystery, he ascends in glory to the right hand of the Father, where he reigns over heaven and earth.

In the third mystery, the descent of the Holy Spirit, we arrive at the hinge of the Glorious Mysteries. Here we reflect on how Christ's work of salvation in his resurrection and ascension is applied to our lives. Through Christ's Spirit dwelling in our hearts, we share in the life of the risen and ascended Jesus.

The last two glorious mysteries get us to reflect on the one who has been completely filled with the Holy Spirit and already shares in the fullness of Christ's glory: Mary. When we look at her splendor in heaven, we see an icon of what awaits us if we imitate her faithfulness and allow Christ's Spirit to transform our lives. In the Assumption, we contemplate Mary's "enjoying beforehand, by a unique privilege, the destiny reserved for all the just at the resurrection of the dead" (*RVM*, 23). In the last glorious mystery, we ponder Mary being crowned as Queen of Heaven and Earth. While contemplating Mary's participation

in her son's reign, we are reminded of our own royal mission to reign
with Christ over sin and death for the rest of eternity.

. . . .

The First Glorious Mystery
The Resurrection
MATTHEW 28:1–15; MARK 16:1–18; LUKE 24:1–49; JOHN 20:1–21:25

> But on the first day of the week, at early dawn, they went to the
> tomb, taking the spices which they had prepared. And they found
> the stone rolled away from the tomb. (Luke 23:56–24:2)

Imagine what Mary Magdalene and the other holy women were going
through when they went to Jesus's tomb at the crack of dawn. These are
the women who remained with him during his final hours on Calvary.
They witnessed his body being taken down from the cross, wrapped in
fine linen, and quickly laid in a tomb before the Sabbath rest began that
evening.

Now it is the Sunday morning
after Jesus died, and the Sabbath
has ended. These faithful women
are the first to return to the tomb.

"Even though they abandoned him
on Good Friday, Jesus still views
the apostles as his brothers."

They are in mourning, and they bring spices so they can anoint the
body that was buried hastily on Good Friday. They have no idea that
they are about to become the first witnesses to the most important event
in the history of the world.

Upon their arrival, the women discover that the large stone that
enclosed the tomb has been rolled away. Matthew's Gospel explains
what has happened overnight: "There was a great earthquake; for an
angel of the Lord descended from heaven and came and rolled back
the stone" (Matthew 28:2). The angel's appearance "was like lightning
and his raiment white as snow," and it threw the Roman soldiers who
guarded the tomb into a state of shock. "And for fear of him the guards

trembled and *became like dead men*" (Matthew 28:4, emphasis added). Notice the irony: The very ones who were supposed to be guarding the tomb of a dead man have now become like dead men themselves, while the body of the crucified Christ has risen.

The women do not understand all this yet. At least from the perspective of Luke's Gospel, they only know that the large stone has been moved from the doorway and that the tomb is now open. Imagine their surprise when they walk into the tomb. Expecting to find the corpse of Jesus, the women instead discover two men "in dazzling apparel," angels of the Lord (Luke 24:4–6; see Acts 1:10).

Amazed at all that has taken place this early morning—the rolled-away stone, the missing body, and now two angels appearing—the women respond in fear, bowing their faces to the ground before the heavenly messengers. The angels quickly address the women's bewilderment about the missing body: "Why do you seek the living among the dead? He is not here, but has risen" (Luke 24:5).

STILL BROTHERS

The women's realization of Christ's resurrection reaches a climax when they see the risen Lord himself. On their way back from the tomb, Mary Magdalene and "the other Mary" (the mother of James) become the first to encounter the resurrected Jesus.

> They departed quickly from the tomb with fear and great joy.... And behold, Jesus met them and said, "Hail!" And they came up and took hold of his feet and worshiped him. Then Jesus said to them, "Do not be afraid; go and tell my brethren to go to Galilee, and there they will see me." (Matthew 28:8–10)

The truth of the Resurrection is now confirmed by their seeing the risen Christ for themselves. In awe, the women grasp his feet—an expression of homage one would give to a king. The only way they can respond to the resurrected Jesus is to fall down at his feet and worship him.

What is perhaps most striking in this scene is that Jesus calls the apostles "my brethren." Even though they abandoned him on Good Friday, Jesus still views the apostles as his brothers. We can see this even more clearly when Christ appears to the apostles for the first time later that day.

An Unexpected Peace

On the evening of that day, the first day of the week, the doors being shut where the disciples were, for fear of the Jews, Jesus came and stood among them and said to them, "Peace be with you." When he had said this, he showed them his hands and his side. Then the disciples were glad when they saw the Lord. Jesus said to them again, "Peace be with you." (John 20:19–21)

Christ's first words to the frightened, cowardly apostles in hiding are "Peace be with you." This is no pious throwaway line, nor a simple greeting. In the biblical Hebrew understanding, peace—*shalom*—means "right relationships." It is not simply about avoiding war and fighting. *Shalom* signifies harmonious friendship, covenant intimacy, a relationship of trust. The risen Christ offers the apostles this *shalom*. Perhaps he wishes to make it clear that he has risen not to issue condemnation but to offer them forgiveness and assurance of his friendship.

This is astonishing. Think about what has happened between Jesus and the apostles in the seventy-two hours leading up to Easter. After sharing the Passover, these closest friends of Jesus could not stay awake and pray with him in his moment of great agony in the garden. When he was arrested, these men abandoned him. When the crowds condemned Jesus to death, none of these men came to his defense. When he was carrying his cross, they were nowhere to be found. In their cowardice, all but one let their master die on his own. A greater display of disloyalty and abandonment could hardly be imagined.

Yet Jesus says to these failed men, "Peace be with you." In offering them forgiveness, Jesus does not simply sweep everything under the rug. He does not say, "I'm OK, you're OK. It's no big deal." He seeks them out, comes through their closed doors, and shows them the nail marks in his hands and the piercing from the lance in his side. Jesus will not let the disciples run from their tragic decisions on Good Friday.[1]

The disciples must come to terms with the awful truth about their actions and lack of action, about what they have done and what they have failed to do. And it is precisely in this humbling moment of facing their weaknesses and failings that they receive Jesus's forgiveness and restored friendship. He offers them *shalom*.

BEHIND CLOSED DOORS

This scene highlights what may be one of the most unique aspects of Christianity. While a number of modern religious trends focus on man's search for God, Christianity is much more about God's search for us. Just as he did on Easter Sunday, Jesus continuously seeks us out. Sometimes we push him to the side of our lives or run away from him. Sometimes we hide from God's call or close doors in our hearts, afraid to let Jesus enter certain areas of our lives. But Jesus will not let us stay in hiding for long. Sooner or later, he will allow us to experience the emptiness, anxiety, and unhappiness that come from a life not centered on him. He will allow us to face our fears, brokenness, and failings.

Jesus wants to pass through the doors and meet us in the dark crevices of our existence—in our insecurities, our doubts, our weaknesses, and our sins. He wants us to come to terms with what we have done and what we have failed to do. He wants us to face the truth about who we really are.

But Jesus comes not to point fingers and condemn. He comes to offer forgiveness, healing, and a new way of life in him. He comes to offer *shalom*.

The Mystery of Easter

This is simply the pattern of salvation found in the mission of the Son of God, who descended into our humanity in order to heal us and raise us up to share in his divinity. In the Incarnation, the Almighty God descended to earth and became a man, entering the broken human family. Throughout his public ministry, the all-holy Son of God continued to lower himself, journeying to the darkest corners of Israel. He did not stay in the temple with the religious elite but associated with lepers, the sick, prostitutes, and other sinners. By speaking with them, touching them, and sharing meals with them, Jesus united himself to the outcasts of first-century Judaism. Meeting them at their lowest points, he healed them, forgave them, and restored them to the Father.

This descent of God is seen especially on Good Friday. At the cross, we encounter most vividly the mystery of the God who relentlessly seeks his people who have run away. At Calvary, we see Jesus descend into the depths of our sufferings, sinfulness, and estrangement from the Father. And it is precisely at that point that he finds us.

By meeting us at the lowest point of our existence, the Son of God, who is perfectly united to the Father, is able to transform our weak, fallen humanity and lift it up with him in his resurrection. The all-holy Son of God unites himself to our utter brokenness on Good Friday so he can raise us up with him on Easter Sunday. In the Resurrection, Jesus offers the fallen human family a restored relationship with the Father. Indeed, the risen Christ offers us *shalom*.

....

The Second Glorious Mystery
The Ascension
Acts 1:1–11; Mark 16:19–20; Luke 24:50–53

To them he presented himself alive after his passion by many proofs, appearing to them during forty days, and speaking of the kingdom of God. (Acts 1:3)

This verse from Acts sets the context for Christ's ascension. It is significant that Jesus has been appearing to the apostles and talking to them about the kingdom for *forty days* after his resurrection. For the ancient Israelites, the number forty would symbolize a time of intense training and preparation for some great work. It recalls, for example, the forty years Israel spent in the desert preparing to enter the Promised Land and the forty days Moses fasted on Mount Sinai when receiving the Ten Commandments.

Most of all, these forty days parallel Jesus's fast in the desert before he was led by the Spirit to begin proclaiming the kingdom in Galilee (see Luke 4:14). In the same way, he now spends forty days preparing the apostles to be led by the Holy Spirit at Pentecost, when they will begin their ministry to the ends of the earth.

THE KINGDOM QUESTION

So when they had come together, they asked him, "Lord, will you at this time restore the kingdom to Israel?" (Acts 1:6)

The apostles ask an excellent question. After all, if Jesus is the son of David and the Messiah-King, he must be the one who will rebuild the Davidic dynasty, which has been lying in ruins for centuries. Although foreign powers have controlled the people of Israel for much of the last six hundred years, the prophets foretold that the kingdom eventually would be reconstituted and become even more glorious than it was in the days of David and Solomon. Not only would this kingdom reunite Israel, but it also would gather all peoples to worship the one true God.

At the Last Supper, Jesus spoke of this renewed Israel and of the apostles playing a leadership role in it (see Luke 22:29–30). Now, after having spent forty days in training with the resurrected King talking about the kingdom, the apostles anxiously wait for their mission to begin. That is why they ask if now is the time for the kingdom to be restored.

To the End of the Earth

He said to them, "It is not for you to know times or seasons which the Father has fixed by his own authority. But you shall receive power when the Holy Spirit has come upon you; and you shall be my witnesses in Jerusalem and in all Judea and Samaria and to the end of the earth" (Acts 1:7–8)

At first glance, it may seem as if Jesus is avoiding the apostles' question. He says, "It is not for you to know times or seasons." However, he does affirm the coming of the kingdom's restoration and calls on the apostles to play a crucial role in it. In fact, in these words, Jesus gives the apostles their marching orders. He tells them they will be his witnesses "in *Jerusalem* and in all *Judea* and *Samaria* and to the *end of the earth.*"

"Like the first apostles, we too share in the mission of spreading Christ's kingdom in the world today."

On one level, these words provide an itinerary for their mission and an outline for the rest of the Acts of the Apostles: Their proclamation of the kingdom will begin in *Jerusalem* (see Acts 2–7), move out to the regions of *Judea* and *Samaria* (Acts 8–12), and then spread throughout much of the known world, even to the capital city of Rome (Acts 13–28).

On another level, by announcing the apostles' mission to go out to all the nations, Jesus answers their kingdom question. He says that *they* will be the ones to fulfill the worldwide mission of the kingdom. In fact, the kingdom will be restored and its universal reign extended precisely through their own witness to the Gospel, from Jerusalem to the ends of the earth.

A Cloud of Glory

And when he had said this, as they were looking on, he was lifted up, and a cloud took him out of their sight. And while they were gazing into heaven as he went, behold, two men stood by them in white robes, and said, "Men of Galilee, why do you stand looking into heaven? This Jesus, who was taken up from you into heaven, will come in the same way as you saw him go into heaven." (Acts 1:9–11)

Many times throughout salvation history, God has manifested his divine presence to Israel in the form of a cloud. It was God's cloud of glory that filled the sanctuary in the desert, filled the temple in Jerusalem, and overshadowed Christ during his transfiguration. Now a cloud of glory lifts Jesus up and brings him to heaven in triumph (see 1 Timothy 3:16).

Christ's return to the Father on a cloud also signals the fulfillment of an important prophecy from the Old Testament. The prophet Daniel had a vision of a "son of man" figure who appeared victorious over his enemies and was carried to God on "the clouds of heaven" to receive a worldwide kingdom that would last forever:

> I saw in the night visions,
> and behold, with the clouds of heaven
>   there came one like a son of man,
> and he came to the Ancient of Days
>   and was presented before him.
> And to him was given dominion
>   and glory and kingdom,
> that all peoples, nations, and languages
>   should serve him;
> his dominion is an everlasting dominion,
>   which shall not pass away,
> and his kingdom one
>   that shall not be destroyed. (Daniel 7:13–14)

Jesus is the "son of man" who in his exaltation is presented before God the Father, the Ancient of Days, and is given an everlasting kingdom that will reign over all nations (see *CCC*, 664). As such, Christ's ascension may provide a further response to the apostles' question, "When will the kingdom be restored to Israel?" By rising to the Father on a cloud of glory, Jesus confirms that he is the Son of Man who has emerged victorious and that the restored kingdom Daniel envisioned has arrived. It is now up to the apostles to extend this kingdom to the ends of the earth.

Our Mission

Like the first apostles, we too share in the mission of spreading Christ's kingdom in the world today. Yet we do not have to become missionaries in Africa to do this. Whether a teacher in the classroom, a businessman in the workplace, a college student on campus, or a mother raising children in the home, all Christians play a crucial role in helping build the kingdom where God has called them to serve. By bringing the extraordinary witness of Christian truth, virtue, and love into our ordinary, daily endeavors, we can help transform our culture into the kingdom of the risen and ascended Christ.

It is true that the apostles were charged to go out to the end of the earth, but they had to start with their own people, right in their own capital city of Jerusalem. We too do not have to look very far to find places where the truth of the Gospel and Christ's love are desperately needed. Let us consider what more we can do to imitate the apostles and begin our mission right in our own country, bringing Christ into our workplaces, our parishes, our schools, our neighborhoods, and most of all, our own homes.

··

The Third Glorious Mystery

The Descent of the Holy Spirit

ACTS 2:1–41

When the day of Pentecost had come, they were all together in one place. (Acts 2:1)

Pentecost originally was not a Christian feast but a Jewish one. Each year, on the fiftieth day after Passover, the Jews celebrated Pentecost as an agricultural festival. Many would make a pilgrimage to Jerusalem to offer the "first fruits" from the wheat harvest.

> "The gift of Pentecost, the indwelling of the Holy Spirit, makes all the difference in the world."

Eventually Pentecost took on greater theological meaning, as the Jews associated it with the giving of the Law at Mount Sinai. On this mountain, God gave the people the Ten Commandments and established Israel as his covenant people. According to the book of Exodus, the Jews arrived at Mount Sinai about a month and a half after the first Passover in Egypt (see Exodus 12:1–3; 19:1). Since they celebrated Pentecost each year at about that time, this feast day began to commemorate the giving of the covenant at Sinai and the founding of Israel as God's chosen people.

This background helps us understand what the apostles are doing in Jerusalem. They are gathered together for the Jewish Feast of Pentecost (see Acts 2:1). It also helps us appreciate how fitting it is that God chose to send the Holy Spirit to the apostles on this particular day. Just as Pentecost celebrated the beginning of the old covenant with Israel, so now this day marks the start of the new covenant era with the Church.

A NEW SINAI

And suddenly a sound came from heaven like the rush of a mighty wind, and it filled all the house where they were sitting. And there appeared to them tongues as of fire, distributed and resting on each one of them. And they were all filled with the Holy Spirit and began to speak in other tongues, as the Spirit gave them utterance. (Acts 2:2–4)

This scene of the Holy Spirit falling upon the apostles on the mountain of Jerusalem is reminiscent of the way God appeared to the Israelites on that other famous mountain, Mount Sinai. Just before giving the Ten Commandments, the Lord descended on Sinai in the form of *fire*. This was accompanied by the *loud sound* of a trumpet blast and God's speaking to Moses in thunder (see Exodus 19:16–19). Furthermore, at least one strand of Jewish tradition describes God communicating to the Israelites at Sinai through fire in a *language familiar to the people*. Philo of Alexandria, a first-century Jewish writer, said:

> And a voice sounded forth out of the midst of the fire which had flowed from heaven, a most marvelous and awful voice, the flame being endowed with articulate speech in a language familiar to the hearers, which expressed its words with such clearness and distinctness that the people seemed rather to be seeing than hearing it.[2]

This seems to parallel what happens when the Holy Spirit comes upon the apostles in Jerusalem on Pentecost.[3] Just as the old covenant was established at Sinai about a month and a half after the first Passover lambs were sacrificed in Egypt, so now the new covenant is established with the Church about a month and a half after the true Passover Lamb was sacrificed on the cross. And just as God descended on Mount Sinai in the form of fire, with a loud sound and with divine speech familiar to the people, so now God's Holy Spirit descends on the mountain of Jerusalem with the extraordinary signs of *fire*, a *loud sound*, and *miraculous speech that is understood by people of different languages*. Portrayed as a new Sinai event, the descent of the Holy Spirit at Pentecost marks another turning point in salvation history, the birth of the new covenant people of God, the Church.

A New Kind of Law

Amid these many parallels, we can see that what is given in the new covenant (the Holy Spirit) far surpasses what was given in the old covenant (the Law). Even though Israel received the Ten Commandments at Sinai, the rest of the Old Testament story clearly shows that the nation constantly failed to keep them. The lesson we learn from the Scriptures is that the Law by itself is not enough.

And if we are honest, most of us realize this from our own personal experience. Simply *knowing* what is right does not always mean we will *do* what is right. How many times have we known we should do something good but failed to do it? How many times have we known we should avoid saying or doing something but find ourselves saying or doing it anyway? With St. Paul, we can humbly admit our utter weakness: "I do not understand my own actions. For I do not do what I want, but I do the very thing I hate.... For I do not do the good I want, but the evil I do not want is what I do" (Romans 7:15, 19).

The problem is not simply that people do not know the Law but that they cannot keep the Law on their own power. This is why the prophets foretold that God would establish a new covenant with a new kind of law: a law that would be written on people's hearts. This new law would do much more than inform people of a moral code they should follow. It would actually give people a supernatural strength to rise above their weak, fallen human nature and walk in God's ways.

The book of Jeremiah, for example, describes the contrast between the old law, which Israel broke, and the interior law, which would come in the new covenant era:

> Behold, the days are coming, says the Lord, when I will make a new covenant with the house of Israel and the house of Judah, not like the covenant which I made with their fathers when I took them by the hand to bring them out of the land of Egypt, my covenant

which they broke.... But this is the covenant which I will make with the house of Israel after those days, says the Lord: I will put my law within them, and I will write it upon their hearts; I will be their God, and they shall be my people. (Jeremiah 31:31–33)

What is important for our reflection on Pentecost is that the prophet Ezekiel associates this new law with God's own Spirit dwelling in us, transforming our hard hearts and strengthening us to follow God's ways: "A new heart I will give you, and a new spirit I will put within you; and I will take out of your flesh the heart of stone and give you a heart of flesh. And I will put my spirit within you, and cause you to walk in my statutes" (Ezekiel 36:26–27).

Changing Our Hearts of Stone

With the Holy Spirit descending on the people at Pentecost, this third glorious mystery stands as a fulfillment of Jeremiah's and Ezekiel's prophecies about the new covenant. While the old law was written by the finger of God on tablets of stone, the new law is written by God's Holy Spirit on the hearts of believers, prompting them to love as Christ loved, turning them away from sin, and giving them the power to fulfill the law, which they could not keep on their own (see 2 Corinthians 3:3; Romans 8:1–4; *CCC*, 733–736).

This gift of Pentecost, the indwelling of the Holy Spirit, makes all the difference in the world. Indeed, with Christ's Spirit we can love our God, our spouse, our children, our coworkers, and our friends in a way that rises above our own selfish, proud, fearful human nature. When Christ's Spirit works through us, his generosity transforms our selfishness, his humility softens our pride, and his courage overcomes our timidity. When we allow the Holy Spirit to change our hearts of stone and permeate our lives, we can truly say, "It is no longer I who live, but Christ who lives in me" (Galatians 2:20).

A REVERSAL OF BABEL

Now there were dwelling in Jerusalem Jews, devout men from every nation under heaven. And at this sound the multitude came together, and they were bewildered, because each one heard them speaking in his own language. And they were amazed and wondered, saying, "Are not all these who are speaking Galileans? And how is it that we hear, each of us in his own native language?" (Acts 2:5–8).

Jews and gentile converts to Judaism from all over the Roman Empire are gathered in Jerusalem for Pentecost (see Acts 2:5–10). Expecting simply to participate in this Jewish pilgrimage feast, they end up experiencing much more than they ever imagined. They witness the descent of the Holy Spirit and become some of the first converts to Christianity.

Filled with the Holy Spirit, Peter delivers his first sermon, proclaiming the death and resurrection of the Messiah. At the end of his speech, he challenges the people: "Repent, and be baptized every one of you in the name of Jesus Christ for the forgiveness of your sins; and you shall receive the gift of the Holy Spirit" (Acts 2:38). About three thousand come to believe in the Gospel and are baptized that day (see Acts 2:41).

Pentecost serves as a preview of things to come. Many from this international gathering of Jews and gentile converts hear the Gospel, believe, and are baptized on Pentecost. This scene in Jerusalem anticipates what will happen across the world. Many Jews and gentiles throughout the Roman empire will hear the Gospel preached by the apostles. They too will believe, be baptized, and be gathered into Christ's Church.

The fact that each person hears the apostles in his or her own language may signal the reversal of the curse of the Tower of Babel and the reunion of the human family. In Genesis 11, God diversified human language so people could no longer understand each other's speech. This signified the division within the human family sown by sin. The descent of the Holy Spirit overcomes that language barrier, signifying how the new law of the Spirit overcomes sin and reunites the human family in the one family of God, the Church.

The Spirit's action invites us to consider the relationships in our lives that need healing. Do you experience tensions with family members, friends, or work relationships? Ask the Holy Spirit to help bring reconciliation and a deeper peace in those relationships. The same Holy Spirit who brought reconciliation at Pentecost can bring healing to the relationships in your life.

Mary's Prayer for Pentecost

All these with one accord devoted themselves to prayer, together with the women and Mary the mother of Jesus, and with his brethren. (Acts 1:14)

We close this reflection on the third glorious mystery by considering Mary's role in it. The Acts of the Apostles notes that the mother of Jesus gathered with the apostles to pray in the period leading up to Pentecost (see Acts 1:14). Vatican II describes Mary's prayer in these days as a petition for the whole Church to receive the same Holy Spirit that already overshadowed her at the annunciation.[4]

In commenting on this theme, John Paul II once said that Mary's prayer attracts the action of the Holy Spirit in the world. With Mary's "yes" at the annunciation, the Holy Spirit conceived the physical body of Christ in her womb. Now, with Mary's prayerful intercession at Pentecost, the same Spirit descends upon the apostles to form the Mystical Body of Christ, the Church.[5]

Mary's intercession continues to foster the coming of the Holy Spirit in our lives today. Through her maternal care for all Christians, she pleads for that new law of the Spirit to be written deep in our hearts, permeating all our thoughts, desires, words, and actions. May Mary continue to implore Christ's Spirit to transform our weak, self-centered human nature with his infinite, supernatural love.

....

The Fourth Glorious Mystery
The Assumption of Mary
PSALM 132:8; LUKE 1:28; REVELATION 12:1

And a great portent appeared in heaven, a woman clothed with the sun, with the moon under her feet, and on her head a crown of twelve stars. (Revelation 12:1)

What does Catholicism teach about the assumption of Mary? And why is this event contemplated in the fourth glorious mystery? Let us begin by considering a few key points from the *Catechism of the Catholic Church* (see *CCC*, 966).

First, in discussing the assumption, the *Catechism* affirms that Mary did not suffer from original sin but was conceived full of grace. According to this doctrine, known as the Immaculate Conception, God's supernatural life dwelt in Mary from the very beginning of her existence.

It is important to emphasize that from a Catholic perspective, the Immaculate Conception is not simply about Mary. This doctrine, which has its roots in early Christianity, ultimately is about the mystery of Jesus Christ. God became man in Mary's womb. Since Jesus truly is the all-holy God, the Second Person of the Trinity, Catholics believe he is worthy to dwell in a pure vessel, a holy temple. Thus, it is fitting that God would prepare Mary as an immaculate dwelling place, full of grace and not stained by sin, for the God-man.

The annunciation scene in Luke's Gospel may at least point in this direction. The angel Gabriel greets Mary, "Hail, full of grace." The Greek word in Luke's Gospel for "full of grace" (Luke 1:28) is in a perfect passive participle form, which would indicate that Mary already has been filled with God's saving grace, even before Jesus was conceived in her womb.[6] As we will see, the Immaculate Conception will serve as a basis for understanding Mary's assumption.

Mary's Death?

Second, the *Catechism* teaches that Mary was taken to heaven when the course of her earthly life was finished. The Church does not declare whether Mary died and then was assumed into heaven or whether she was assumed before she died. It leaves open both possibilities. However, the majority of theologians and saints throughout the centuries have affirmed that Mary *did* experience death—not as a penalty for sin but in conformity to her son, who willingly experienced death on our behalf. In support of this latter view, John Paul II said, "The Mother is not superior to the Son who underwent death, giving it a new meaning and changing it into a means of salvation."[7]

> "The assumption truly was an act of love, in which Mary's ardent longing to be with her son was finally fulfilled."

Third, the *Catechism* affirms that Mary was taken body and soul into heavenly glory right at the end of her earthly life. One of the consequences of original sin is the corruption of the body (see *CCC*, 400; Genesis 3:19). If Mary was full of grace and did not suffer from original sin, it is fitting that she, like her son, would not experience such bodily corruption.

Biblical Assumptions

Although there are no explicit proof texts in Scripture for Mary's assumption, some biblical themes may at least shed light on this doctrine. For example, the notion of being taken up into heaven has some precedent in Scripture. Enoch was taken into heaven without seeing death (see Hebrews 11:5), and Elijah was whisked into heaven by the chariots of fire at the end of his life (see 2 Kings 2:11). If God could assume these righteous men of the Old Testament, it is certainly possible that Jesus could assume his own mother as well.

Even more, since the Bible presents Mary as the first Christian disciple, it is fitting that she would be the first to receive the blessings of following Christ. In the New Testament, Mary is presented as the first to hear God's word and accept it at the annunciation (see Luke 1:38, 45). She responds to God's word promptly by going in haste to help Elizabeth. She also describes herself as a servant of the Lord (see Luke 1:38, 48).

> "In the ancient Near East, the woman sitting on the throne was not the king's wife but his mother."

Mary remains faithful to her son, following him even to the cross (see John 19:25–27), where she experiences the fulfillment of Simeon's prophecy at the Presentation: "A sword will pierce through your own soul also" (Luke 2:35). She perseveres in faith throughout her life. She gathers with the apostles for prayer even after her son's ascension (see Acts 1:14). Thus, the New Testament presents a clear portrait of Mary as the first and preeminent disciple of Christ, who hears the word of God and keeps it in her heart.

Since one of the blessings promised to all faithful disciples is victory over death, it is fitting that Mary, who is the first and model disciple of Christ, would be the first to receive this blessing. Catholics thus believe that the privilege of resurrection promised to all faithful Christians was given first to Mary and in a totally unique way. While the rest of us hope to have our bodies raised to glory at the end of time, Mary experienced the resurrection and glorification of her body at the moment her earthly life ended. Thus, her assumption—which flows from her unique participation in Christ's victory as the mother of the Savior and as the first and most faithful of Christ's followers—anticipates to some degree our own share in the fullness of that victory if we persevere as followers of Christ.

The Saints and Scripture

Theologians and saints throughout the centuries have seen other Scripture passages and themes shedding light on Mary's assumption. While numerous examples could be considered, let us look briefly at just a few texts Pope Pius XII highlighted in his proclamation of Mary's Assumption in 1950.[8]

The pope notes Psalm 132, which celebrates the ark of the covenant being brought by David to the temple in Jerusalem: "Arise, O Lord, and go to your resting place, you and the ark of your might" (Psalm 132:8). Since Mary is like a new ark of the covenant carrying God's presence in her womb, some have seen these words as prefiguring Mary's assumption. Just as David transferred the ark to its rest in the Jerusalem temple of old, so now Jesus, the true son of David, brings Mary, the new ark of the covenant, to her final resting place in heaven.

Moreover, some have looked upon "the Ark of the Covenant, built of incorruptible wood and placed in the Lord's temple, as a type of the most pure body of the Virgin Mary, preserved and exempted from all the corruption of the tomb and raised up to such glory in heaven."[9]

Pope Pius XII also notes how others have turned to the fourth commandment, "Honor your father and your mother" (Exodus 20:12), as a source for understanding Mary's assumption. These would say that if Jesus observed the fourth commandment perfectly, he would honor his mother by assuming her into heaven at the end of her life. Along similar lines, St. Francis de Sales once said, "What son would not bring his mother back to life and would not bring her into paradise after her death if he could?"[10]

Another text commonly used to shed light on Mary's assumption is Revelation 12:1, which presents "a woman clothed with the sun" appearing in heaven as a sign. In this apocalyptic vision, the woman gives birth to a male child who is described as the Messiah, ruling all nations with a rod of iron and carried up to the throne of God (see Revelation 12:5; Psalm 2:9). While we will treat this passage more in our reflection on the fifth glorious mystery, we can say here that since the male child is generally understood to be the Messiah, the woman giving birth to this child can be seen as Mary. Catholics often have seen in this vision support for Mary's assumption, by which she was clothed in God's glory and began her heavenly reign.

An Event of Love

Finally, let us consider what a moment the Assumption must have been for Mary! In describing this scene, some Church Fathers spoke of Jesus himself coming back to earth to take his mother and bring her to her heavenly home. More recently, John Paul II said that the Assumption truly was an event of love, in which Mary's ardent longing to be with her son was finally fulfilled. In fact, many paintings of the Assumption portray Mary rising in splendor on a cloud to heaven, received by the angels with trumpets and celebration, and reunited joyfully with her beloved son.

While artistic depictions of this triumphant event in Mary's life are often celebrated, not as well-known are the many pieces of art that portray her last moments on earth, just before her assumption. Yet such a depiction of the end of Mary's life—her moment between heaven and earth—can be found on one of the main doors of St. Peter's Basilica in Rome. There Mary is surprisingly portrayed as *falling*, as if she were definitively letting go of all the trials and sufferings of this life and allowing herself to fall asleep. Indeed, she is letting go of life itself as she passes from this world to the next. It is just at this moment of abandoning herself into the Father's hands that the angels rush down to catch her and bring her up to heaven.

This depiction captures an aspect of Mary's assumption that offers us hope in the midst of our trials in this "valley of tears." This is the hope that God will carry us through our distress and lift up our heavy hearts. So take a moment right now and ask yourself, what burdens, troubles, and worries are weighing you down? How can you entrust yourself more to God's loving care?

With whatever we're facing in life, may we, like Mary, fall into the Father's arms, so that we may have a more profound experience of his supporting us in our present sufferings and raising us to himself—both now and at the hour of our death.

···

The Fifth Glorious Mystery
The Crowning of Mary
LUKE 1:43; REVELATION 12:1

At your right hand stands the queen in gold of Ophir. (Psalm 45:9)

For many Christians today, it is not obvious why Mary should be called a queen. After all, she is not the wife of Christ the King but his mother. Yet from a biblical perspective, Mary's queenship would make a lot of sense.

In the ancient Near East, the woman sitting on the throne in the kingdom was not the king's wife but his mother. Most kings in this period had large harems. King Solomon, for example, had seven hundred wives and three hundred concubines (see 1 Kings 11:3). It would have been impossible to bestow the queenship on a thousand women! Yet, while the king might have had multiple wives, he only had one mother; thus, the queenship was given to her.

The Scriptures attest to the important role of the queen mother in ancient Israel. She held an official position in the royal court, participating in her son's reign over the people. She was described as having a throne and a crown (see 1 Kings 2:19; Jeremiah 13:18) and serving as a counselor to her royal son (see Proverbs 31:1). The queen mother was one of the first mentioned in the list of palace officials (see 2 Kings 24:12), and in the narrative of 1 and 2 Kings, she almost always is introduced by name whenever a new king assumes the throne. Most of all, the queen mother served as an advocate for the people, receiving petitions and presenting them to her royal son (see 1 Kings 2:19).

A ROYAL ADVOCATE

We can see the importance of the queen mother by contrasting two scenes in the life of Bathsheba, which show her role when she was simply the wife of King David and her role as queen mother, when her son Solomon was on the throne. When David was still the king and Bathsheba entered the royal chamber, she had to bow with her face to the ground and pay him homage, saying, "May my lord King David live for ever" (1 Kings 1:16, 31). We find a very different picture once Solomon becomes king and Bathsheba steps into the office of queen mother.

A man named Adonijah recognizes Bathsheba's powerful position as advocate and asks her to bring a petition to her royal son. Knowing that the king always listens to the intercession of the queen mother, Adonijah confidently says to her, "Please ask King Solomon—*he will not refuse you*" (1 Kings 2:17).

Bathsheba agrees to bring the petition to the king. However, when she enters the royal chamber this time as queen mother, her experience is entirely different compared to the last time she was there. Instead of Bathsheba having to pay homage to the king, King Solomon stands up and bows down before *her*. Even more, the king has a throne brought for her at his right hand, symbolizing her position of authority.

When Bathsheba says she has a petition to present to Solomon, he responds, "Make your request, my mother; for I will not refuse you" (1 Kings 2:19–20). With these words, Solomon affirms his commitment to the queen mother's intercessory role as advocate in the kingdom.[11]

"Mother of My Lord"

All this is important background to understanding the royal office of the mother of Christ. Jesus is the new Son of David, the Messiah-King who fulfills all the promises given to the Davidic kingdom. If in the Jewish, biblical worldview of the Davidic kingdom the king's mother reigned as queen, then the mother of the new Davidic king, Jesus, clearly would be understood as the new queen mother.

That seems to be what Elizabeth affirms in the visitation scene. Filled with the Holy Spirit, she greets the mother of Jesus, saying, "Why is this granted me, that the mother of my Lord should come to me?" (Luke 1:43). The title Elizabeth bestows on Mary is charged with royal significance. In the royal court language of the ancient Near East, the title "mother of my Lord" would have been used to address the queen mother, for "my lord" was a title of honor for the king himself (see 2 Samuel 24:21). In calling Mary "mother of my Lord," Elizabeth acknowledges her as the mother of the king, as queen mother.

A Woman Clothed with the Sun

We return to a passage in Revelation 12 to see the light it sheds on Mary's royal office:

> And a great sign appeared in heaven, a woman clothed with the sun, with the moon under her feet, and on her head a crown of twelve stars.... She brought forth a male child, one who is to rule all the nations with a rod of iron, but her child was caught up to God and to his throne. (Revelation 12:1, 5)

Who is this mysterious woman appearing in such royal splendor, clothed with the sun, with the moon under her feet, and crowned with twelve stars? The key to unlocking the mystery of this queenly woman can be found in the identity of the child she bears. Revelation 12 tells us that the woman gives birth to a male child who "rules all the nations with a rod of iron" (Revelation 12:5).

This description of the child is significant because it is taken directly from the messianic Psalm 2. In this psalm, God foretells how he will rescue the Messiah-King from his enemies and establish for him a reign over all the earth:

Ask of me, and I will make the nations your heritage,

and the ends of the earth your possession.

You shall break them with a rod of iron. (Psalm 2:8–9)

Since the book of Revelation portrays the male child with this messianic imagery from Psalm 2, the child would be seen as the long-awaited Messiah-King. And who is the royal woman who gave birth to the Messiah? Clearly that woman is Mary.[12]

In Revelation 12, Mary appears in all her majesty, reigning in heaven alongside her royal son. Indeed, she is the queen mother of Christ's everlasting kingdom. Like the queen mothers of old, she wears a crown on her head, symbolizing her regal office. The twelve stars on her crown express her reign over the Church, which is born from the twelve tribes of Israel and founded on the twelve apostles. Clothed with the sun, she radiates God's glory. With the moon under her feet, she appears in royal authority, since "under the feet" imagery symbolized regal power and defeat of one's enemies (see Psalm 8:6; 110:1).

Finally, the combination of the sun, moon, and stars imagery may recall the famous dream of the patriarch Joseph. In this vision, Joseph saw the sun, moon, and eleven stars bowing down before him (see Genesis 37:9). This dream foreshadowed how Joseph would rule over his father, mother, and eleven brothers when he rose to the second highest position in Pharaoh's kingdom in Egypt. The similar images describing Mary in Revelation 12 may highlight her own royal authority as she assumes one of the most important offices in Christ's kingdom, that of the queen mother.

"I Will Not Refuse You"

With all this background, we are still left wondering, what does Mary's queenship *mean*? Is this a throwback to an outdated governmental structure? Is her queenship simply a figurehead position?

To understand Mary's royal office, we must view it from within the biblical perspective of Christ's kingdom, not secular monarchies. Jesus himself emphasized that his kingdom "is not of this world" (John 18:36). Unlike the pagan rulers who use their authority to serve themselves, Jesus said he exercises his authority "not to be served but to serve" (Matthew 20:28).

Mary, the faithful servant of the Lord, participates in his kingdom in this same way. Indeed, in Christ's kingdom, to serve is to reign. And Mary reigns as queen by serving as a royal advocate for God's people. Like the queen mothers in the Davidic kingdom, Mary stands as a powerful intercessor for the people in Christ's kingdom today.

John Paul II points out that Mary lovingly presents our needs and petitions before Christ's throne and so serves the kingdom by leading souls closer to her son:

> Thus, far from creating distance between her and us, Mary's glorious state as queen brings about a continuous and caring closeness. She knows everything that happens in our lives and supports us with maternal love in our trials. Taken up to heavenly glory, Mary dedicates herself totally to the work of salvation. She wants every living person to know the happiness granted to her. She is a queen who gives all that she possesses, participating above all in the life and love of Christ.[13]

In this last mystery of the rosary, let us give thanks for the loving intercession of Mary, our queen mother. May we confidently turn to Mary with our needs, knowing that she presents our petitions before her royal son and trusting that Jesus responds to her as Solomon did to Bathsheba, "Make your request, my mother; for I will not refuse you" (1 Kings 2:20).

Group Study Questions

1. Pope St. John Paul II offers the rosary as a "prayer for peace" (*RVM*, 6, 40). How does the *shalom* that Jesus gives differ from the peace the world tries to give? How can your prayer of the rosary bring Jesus's peace to yourself, your family, your other relationships, and the world?

2. Pope St. John Paul II says of the third glorious mystery, the descent of the Holy Spirit, "Pentecost...reveals the face of the Church as a family gathered together with Mary, enlivened by the powerful outpouring of the Spirit and ready for the mission of evangelization" (*RVM*, 23). Why can this mystery be called "the hinge" of the Glorious Mysteries?

3. How does Mary's last moment on earth (just before her assumption) inspire us to entrust our cares and trials to the Lord more?

4. The rosary begins with Mary (in the first joyful mystery, the annunciation) and ends with her assumption and her crowning as Queen of Heaven (fourth and fifth glorious mysteries). What might this say about her place in God's plan of redemption?

CHAPTER TWELVE

A Scriptural Rosary

This section provides readers with a practical tool to help incorporate more Scripture in their praying of the rosary. In what is commonly known as a "scriptural rosary," we offer for each mystery ten short lines from the Bible.

As we saw in chapter 7, St. John Paul II encourages us to begin each decade of the rosary with a reading from Scripture. This helps prepare our minds to contemplate the mystery at hand. The biblical verses in this scriptural rosary can serve as a resource to help nourish our contemplation. One or two verses given here can be recited out loud or reflected on quietly at the start of each decade. Having ten Scripture verses available for each decade may help free the mind from worrying about locating a mystery in the Bible every time an Our Father bead approaches. Also, since there are ten verses to choose from, different aspects of the mystery can be chosen for reflection each time the rosary is prayed.

Another way these verses can be used is in a traditional scriptural rosary, in which a Bible verse is read before each Hail Mary. For example, in the first joyful mystery, the annunciation, the first Scripture verse is read: "In the sixth month the angel Gabriel was sent from God." Then the first Hail Mary is recited. A second verse is read before the second Hail Mary, and so on throughout each decade. This approach is similar to the way the rosary was sometimes prayed in its early days—with one meditation point from Christ's life being contemplated with each Hail Mary (as discussed in chapter 6).

Selecting only ten short lines from Scripture for each of the mysteries is a challenging task. Some were chosen, while other inspiring ones were left out. In order to draw the connection between this scriptural rosary and the rest of this book, the verses discussed in the biblical reflections on the mysteries in chapters 8 through 11 were given priority. Those reflections, therefore, help illumine the scriptural rosary that follows.

Finally, it must be said that there are many ways one could present a scriptural rosary, and the particular model offered here in no way is meant to be all-encompassing. It is simply intended to serve as a tool that an individual, family, or group could use to encounter the mysteries of the rosary in Sacred Scripture.

THE FIRST JOYFUL MYSTERY

THE ANNUNCIATION

1. In the sixth month the angel Gabriel was sent from God to…a virgin betrothed to a man whose name was Joseph…and the virgin's name was Mary (Luke 1:26–27). *Hail Mary…*

2. And he came to her and said, "Hail, full of grace, the Lord is with you!" (Luke 1:28). *Hail Mary…*

3. But she was greatly troubled at the saying, and considered in her mind what sort of greeting this might be (Luke 1:29). *Hail Mary…*

4. And the angel said to her, "Do not be afraid, Mary, for you have found favor with God" (Luke 1:30). *Hail Mary…*

5. "And behold, you will conceive in your womb and bear a son, and you shall call his name Jesus" (Luke 1:31). *Hail Mary…*

6. "He will be great, and will be called the Son of the Most High;… and he will reign over the house of Jacob for ever" (Luke 1:32–33). *Hail Mary…*

7. And Mary said to the angel, "How can this be, since I have no husband?" (Luke 1:34). *Hail Mary…*

8. And the angel said to her, "The Holy Spirit will come upon you, and the power of the Most High will overshadow you" (Luke 1:35). *Hail Mary…*

9. "Therefore the child to be born will be called holy, the Son of God" (Luke 1:35). *Hail Mary…*

10. "Behold, I am the handmaid of the Lord; let it be to me according to your word" (Luke 1:38). *Hail Mary…*

THE SECOND JOYFUL MYSTERY
THE VISITATION

1. In those days Mary arose and went with haste into the hill country, to a city of Judah, and she entered the house of Zechariah and greeted Elizabeth (Luke 1:39–40). *Hail Mary…*

2. And when Elizabeth heard the greeting of Mary, the babe leaped in her womb (Luke 1:41). *Hail Mary…*

3. Elizabeth was filled with the Holy Spirit and she exclaimed with a loud cry, "Blessed are you among women, and blessed is the fruit of your womb!" (Luke 1:41–42). *Hail Mary…*

4. "And why is this granted me, that the mother of my Lord should come to me?" (Luke 1:43). *Hail Mary…*

5. "For behold, when the voice of your greeting came to my ears, the babe in my womb leaped for joy" (Luke 1:44). *Hail Mary…*

6. "And blessed is she who believed that there would be a fulfillment of what was spoken to her from the Lord" (Luke 1:45). *Hail Mary…*

7. And Mary said, "My soul magnifies the Lord, and my spirit rejoices in God my Savior" (Luke 1:46–47). *Hail Mary…*

8. "For he has regarded the low estate of his handmaiden" (Luke 1:48). *Hail Mary…*

9. "For behold, henceforth all generations will call me blessed" (Luke 1:48). *Hail Mary…*

10. "For he who is mighty has done great things for me, and holy is his name" (Luke 1:49). *Hail Mary…*

THE THIRD JOYFUL MYSTERY
THE NATIVITY

1. And Joseph also went up from Galilee…to the city of David, which is called Bethlehem…to be enrolled with Mary his betrothed, who was with child (Luke 2:4–5). *Hail Mary…*

2. And she gave birth to her first-born son and wrapped him in swaddling cloths and laid him in a manger, because there was no place for them in the inn (Luke 2:7). *Hail Mary…*

3. And in that region there were shepherds out in the field, keeping watch over their flock by night (Luke 2:8). *Hail Mary…*

4. And an angel of the Lord appeared to them, and the glory of the Lord shone around them, and they were filled with fear (Luke 2:9). *Hail Mary…*

5. And the angel said to them, "Be not afraid; for behold, I bring you good news of a great joy…for to you is born this day in the city of David a Savior, who is Christ the Lord" (Luke 2:10–11). *Hail Mary…*

6. And suddenly there was with the angel a multitude of the heavenly host praising God and saying, "Glory to God in the highest, and on earth peace among men with whom he is pleased" (Luke 2:13–14). *Hail Mary…*

7. And they went with haste, and found Mary and Joseph, and the babe lying in a manger (Luke 2:16). *Hail Mary...*

8. Now when Jesus was born...wise men from the East came to Jerusalem, saying, "Where is he who has been born king of the Jews? For we have seen his star in the East, and have come to worship him" (Matthew 2:1–2). *Hail Mary...*

9. And going into the house they saw the child with Mary his mother, and they fell down and worshiped him (Matthew 2:11). *Hail Mary...*

10. But Mary kept all these things, pondering them in her heart (Luke 2:19). *Hail Mary...*

THE FOURTH JOYFUL MYSTERY
THE PRESENTATION OF JESUS

1. And when the time came for their purification...they brought him up to Jerusalem to present him to the Lord (Luke 2:22). *Hail Mary...*

2. Now there was a man...whose name was Simeon, and this man was...looking for the consolation of Israel (Luke 2:25). *Hail Mary...*

3. And it had been revealed to him by the Holy Spirit that he should not see death before he had seen the Lord's Christ (Luke 2:26). *Hail Mary...*

4. When the parents brought in the child Jesus...[Simeon] took him up in his arms and blessed God (Luke 2:27–28). *Hail Mary...*

5. [Simeon] said, "Lord, let now your servant depart in peace, according to your word" (Luke 2:28–29). *Hail Mary...*

6. "For my eyes have seen your salvation which you have prepared in the presence of all peoples, a light for revelation to the Gentiles, and for glory to your people Israel" (Luke 2:30–32). *Hail Mary...*

7. Simeon blessed them and said to Mary, his mother, "Behold, this child is set for the fall and rising of many in Israel, and for a sign that is spoken against" (Luke 2:34). *Hail Mary...*

8. "And a sword will pierce through your own soul also" (Luke 2:35).

9. And there was a prophetess, Anna.... She did not depart from the temple, worshiping with fasting and prayer night and day (Luke 2:36–37). *Hail Mary...*

10. And coming up at that very hour she gave thanks to God, and spoke of him to all who were looking for the redemption of Jerusalem (Luke 2:38). *Hail Mary...*

THE FIFTH JOYFUL MYSTERY

THE FINDING OF THE CHILD JESUS IN THE TEMPLE

1. Now his parents went to Jerusalem every year at the feast of the Passover.... And when the feast was ended, as they were returning, the boy Jesus stayed behind in Jerusalem (Luke 2:41, 43). *Hail Mary...*

2. His parents did not know it, but supposing him to be in the company they went a day's journey (Luke 2:43–44). *Hail Mary...*

3. They sought him among their kinsfolk and acquaintances; and when they did not find him, they returned to Jerusalem, seeking him (Luke 2:44–45). *Hail Mary...*

4. After three days they found him in the temple, sitting among the teachers, listening to them and asking them questions (Luke 2:46). *Hail Mary...*

5. All who heard him were amazed at his understanding and his answers. And when [Mary and Joseph] saw him they were astonished (Luke 2:47–48). *Hail Mary...*

6. His mother said to him, "Son, why have you treated us so? Behold, your father and I have been looking for you anxiously" (Luke 2:48). *Hail Mary...*

7. And he said to them, "How is it that you sought me? Did you not know that I must be in my Father's house?" (Luke 2:49). *Hail Mary...*

8. And they did not understand the saying which he spoke to them (Luke 2:50). *Hail Mary...*

9. And he went down with them and came to Nazareth, and was obedient to them (Luke 2:51). *Hail Mary...*

10. His mother kept all these things in her heart (Luke 2:51). *Hail Mary...*

THE FIRST LUMINOUS MYSTERY
CHRIST'S BAPTISM IN THE JORDAN

1. In those days came John the Baptist, preaching in the wilderness of Judea, "Repent, for the kingdom of heaven is at hand" (Matthew 3:1–2). *Hail Mary...*

2. Then went out to him Jerusalem and all Judea and all the region about the Jordan (Matthew 3:5). *Hail Mary...*

3. They were baptized by him in the river Jordan, confessing their sins (Matthew 3:6). *Hail Mary...*

4. [John said], "I baptize you with water for repentance, but he who is coming after me is mightier than I;... He will baptize you with the Holy Spirit and with fire" (Matthew 3:11). *Hail Mary...*

5. Then Jesus came from Galilee to the Jordan to John, to be baptized by him (Matthew 3:13). *Hail Mary...*

6. John would have prevented him, saying, "I need to be baptized by you, and do you come to me?" (Matthew 3:14). *Hail Mary...*

7. But Jesus answered him, "Let it be so now; for thus it is fitting for us to fulfill all righteousness" (Matthew 3:15). *Hail Mary...*

8. And when Jesus was baptized, he went up immediately from the water, and behold, the heavens were opened (Matthew 3:16). *Hail Mary...*

9. He saw the Spirit of God descending like a dove, and alighting on him (Matthew 3:16). *Hail Mary...*

10. Lo, a voice from heaven, saying, "This is my beloved Son, with whom I am well pleased" (Matthew 3:17). *Hail Mary...*

THE SECOND LUMINOUS MYSTERY
THE WEDDING FEAST AT CANA

1. On the third day there was a marriage at Cana in Galilee, and the mother of Jesus was there; Jesus also was invited to the marriage, with his disciples (John 2:1–2). *Hail Mary...*

2. When the wine failed, the mother of Jesus said to him, "They have no wine" (John 2:3). *Hail Mary...*

3. And Jesus said to her, "O woman, what have you to do with me? My hour has not yet come" (John 2:4). *Hail Mary...*

4. His mother said to the servants, "Do whatever he tells you" (John 2:5). *Hail Mary...*

5. Now six stone jars were standing there, for the Jewish rites of purification, each holding twenty or thirty gallons (John 2:6). *Hail Mary...*

6. Jesus said to them, "Fill the jars with water." And they filled them up to the brim (John 2:7). *Hail Mary...*

7. He said to them, "Now draw some out, and take it to the steward of the feast." So they took it (John 2:8). *Hail Mary...*

8. When the steward of the feast tasted the water now become wine, and did not know where it came from,... the steward of the feast called the bridegroom (John 2:8–9). *Hail Mary...*

9. [The steward] said to him, "Every man serves the good wine first; and when men have drunk freely, then the poor wine; but you have kept the good wine until now" (John 2:10). *Hail Mary...*

10. This, the first of his signs, Jesus did at Cana in Galilee, and manifested his glory; and his disciples believed in him (John 2:11). *Hail Mary...*

THE THIRD LUMINOUS MYSTERY

THE PROCLAMATION OF THE KINGDOM

1. Jesus spoke to them, saying, "I am the light of the world; he who follows me will not walk in darkness, but will have the light of life" (John 8:12). *Hail Mary...*

2. In him [Jesus] was life, and the life was the light of men. The light shines in the darkness, and the darkness has not overcome it. (John 1:4–5). *Hail Mary...*

3. Jesus came into Galilee, preaching the Gospel of God, and saying, "The time is fulfilled, and the kingdom of God is at hand; repent, and believe in the gospel" (Mark 1:14–15). *Hail Mary...*

4. "Therefore do not be anxious, saying, 'What shall we eat?' or 'What shall we drink?' or 'What shall we wear?' For the Gentiles seek all these things; and your heavenly Father knows that you need them all" (Matthew 6:31–32). *Hail Mary...*

5. "But seek first his kingdom and his righteousness, and all these things shall be yours as well" (Matthew 6:33). *Hail Mary...*

6. And Jesus went about all the cities and villages, teaching in their synagogues and preaching the gospel of the kingdom, and healing every disease and infirmity (Matthew 9:35). *Hail Mary...*

7. And behold, they brought to him a paralytic, lying on his bed; and when Jesus saw their faith he said to the paralytic, "Take heart, my son; your sins are forgiven" (Matthew 9:2). *Hail Mary...*

8. Jesus looked up and said to [the woman caught in adultery], "Woman, where are they? Has no one condemned you?" She said, "No one, Lord" (John 8:10–11). *Hail Mary...*

9. And Jesus said, "Neither do I condemn you; go, and do not sin again" (John 8:11). *Hail Mary...*

10. [Jesus] said to [the apostles], "Receive the Holy Spirit. If you forgive the sins of any, they are forgiven; if you retain the sins of any, they are retained" (John 20:22–23). *Hail Mary...*

THE FOURTH LUMINOUS MYSTERY
THE TRANSFIGURATION

1. And after six days Jesus took with him Peter and James and John his brother, and led them up a high mountain apart (Matthew 17:1). *Hail Mary...*

2. And he was transfigured before them, and his face shone like the sun (Matthew 17:2). *Hail Mary...*

3. His garments became white as light (Matthew 17:2). *Hail Mary...*

4. And behold, there appeared to them Moses and Elijah, talking with him (Matthew 17:3). *Hail Mary...*

5. And Peter said to Jesus, "Lord, it is well that we are here; if you wish, I will make three booths here, one for you and one for Moses and one

for Elijah" (Matthew 17:4). *Hail Mary…*

6. He was still speaking, when lo, a bright cloud overshadowed them (Matthew 17:5). *Hail Mary…*

7. A voice from the cloud said, "This is my beloved Son, with whom I am well pleased; listen to him" (Matthew 17:5). *Hail Mary…*

8. When the disciples heard this, they fell on their faces, and were filled with awe (Matthew 17:6). *Hail Mary…*

9. But Jesus came and touched them, saying, "Rise, and have no fear" (Matthew 17:7). *Hail Mary…*

10. And when they lifted up their eyes, they saw no one but Jesus only (Matthew 17:8). *Hail Mary…*

THE FIFTH LUMINOUS MYSTERY

THE INSTITUTION OF THE EUCHARIST

1. Then came the day of Unleavened Bread, on which the passover lamb had to be sacrificed (Luke 22:7). *Hail Mary…*

2. So Jesus sent Peter and John, saying, "Go and prepare the passover for us, that we may eat it" (Luke 22:8). *Hail Mary…*

3. And when the hour came, he sat at table, and the apostles with him (Luke 22:14). *Hail Mary…*

4. And he said to them, "I have earnestly desired to eat this passover with you before I suffer; for I tell you I shall not eat it until it is fulfilled in the kingdom of God" (Luke 2:15–16). *Hail Mary…*

5. And he took a cup, and when he had given thanks he said, "Take this, and divide it among yourselves for I tell you that from now on I shall not drink of the fruit of the vine until the kingdom of God comes" (Luke 22:17–18). *Hail Mary…*

6. And he took bread, and when he had given thanks he broke it and gave it to them, saying, "This is my body which is given for you" (Luke 22: 19). *Hail Mary...*

7. "Do this in remembrance of me" (Luke 22:19). *Hail Mary...*

8. And likewise the cup after supper, saying, "This cup which is poured out for you is the new covenant in my blood" (Luke 22:20). *Hail Mary...*

9. So Jesus said to them..."He who eats my flesh and drinks my blood has eternal life, and I will raise him up at the last day" (John 6:53–54). *Hail Mary...*

10. "For my flesh is food indeed, and my blood is drink indeed. He who eats my flesh and drinks my blood abides in me, and I in him" (John 6:55–56). *Hail Mary...*

THE FIRST SORROWFUL MYSTERY
THE AGONY IN THE GARDEN

1. And he came out, and went, as was his custom, to the Mount of Olives; and the disciples followed him (Luke 22:39). *Hail Mary...*

2. And when he came to the place he said to them, "Pray that you may not enter into temptation" (Luke 22:40). *Hail Mary...*

3. And taking with him Peter and the two sons of Zebedee, he began to be sorrowful and troubled (Matthew 26:37). *Hail Mary...*

4. Then he said to them, "My soul is very sorrowful, even to death; remain here, and watch with me" (Matthew 26:38). *Hail Mary...*

5. And he withdrew from them about a stone's throw, and knelt down and prayed (Luke 22:41). *Hail Mary...*

6. "Father, if you are willing, remove this cup from me; nevertheless not my will, but yours, be done" (Luke 22:42). *Hail Mary...*

7. And there appeared to him an angel from heaven, strengthening him (Luke 22:43). *Hail Mary…*

8. And being in an agony he prayed more earnestly; and his sweat became like great drops of blood falling down upon the ground (Luke 22:44). *Hail Mary…*

9. And when he rose from prayer, he came to the disciples and found them sleeping for sorrow, and he said to them, "Why do you sleep? Rise and pray that you may not enter into temptation" (Luke 22:45–46). *Hail Mary…*

10. "Behold, the hour is at hand, and the Son of man is betrayed into the hands of sinners. Rise, let us be going; see, my betrayer is at hand" (Matthew 26:45–46). *Hail Mary…*

The Second Sorrowful Mystery
The Scourging at the Pillar

1. Now at the feast the governor was accustomed to release for the crowd any one prisoner whom they wanted (Matthew 27:15). *Hail Mary…*

2. And they had then a notorious prisoner, called Barabbas (Matthew 27:16). *Hail Mary…*

3. The governor again said to them, "Which of the two do you want me to release for you?" And they said, "Barabbas" (Matthew 27:21). *Hail Mary…*

4. Pilate said to them, "Then what shall I do with Jesus who is called Christ?" They all said, "Let him be crucified" (Matthew 27:22). *Hail Mary…*

5. So when Pilate saw that he was gaining nothing, but rather that a riot was beginning, he took water and washed his hands before the crowd (Matthew 27:24). *Hail Mary…*

6. [Pilate said], "I am innocent of this righteous man's blood; see to it yourselves" (Matthew 27:24). *Hail Mary...*

7. And all the people answered, "His blood be on us and on our children!" (Matthew 27:25). *Hail Mary...*

8. Then he released for them Barabbas, and having scourged Jesus, delivered him to be crucified (Matthew 27:26). *Hail Mary...*

9. But he was wounded for our transgressions, he was bruised for our iniquities (Isaiah 53:5). *Hail Mary...*

10. Upon him was the chastisement that made us whole, and with his stripes we are healed" (Isaiah 53:5). *Hail Mary...*

THE THIRD SORROWFUL MYSTERY
THE CROWNING WITH THORNS

1. And the soldiers led him away inside the palace (that is, the praetorium); and they called together the whole battalion (Mark 15:16). *Hail Mary...*

2. And they clothed him in a purple cloak (Mark 15:17). *Hail Mary...*

3. And plaiting a crown of thorns they put it on him (Mark 15:17). *Hail Mary...*

4. [They] put a reed in his right hand (Matthew 27:29). *Hail Mary...*

5. And kneeling before him they mocked him, saying, "Hail, King of the Jews!" (Matthew 27:29). *Hail Mary...*

6. [They] struck him with their hands (John 19:3). *Hail Mary...*

7. And they struck his head with a reed (Mark 15:19). *Hail Mary...*

8. And [they] spat upon him (Mark 15:19). *Hail Mary...*

9. And when they had mocked him, they stripped him of the purple cloak, and put his own clothes on him (Mark 15:20). *Hail Mary...*

10. "I gave my back to those who struck me;… I hid not my face from shame and spitting" (Isaiah 50:6). *Hail Mary…*

THE FOURTH SORROWFUL MYSTERY
THE CARRYING OF THE CROSS

1. And [the soldiers] led him out to crucify him (Mark 15:20). *Hail Mary…*

2. And as they led him away, they seized one Simon of Cyrene, who was coming in from the country (Luke 23:26). *Hail Mary…*

3. [They] laid on him the cross, to carry it behind Jesus (Luke 23:26). *Hail Mary…*

4. And there followed him a great multitude of the people, and of women who bewailed and lamented him (Luke 23:27). *Hail Mary…*

5. But Jesus turning to them said, "Daughters of Jerusalem, do not weep for me, but weep for yourselves and for your children" (Luke 23:28). *Hail Mary…*

6. "For behold, the days are coming when they will say, 'Blessed are the barren, and the wombs that never bore, and the breasts that never gave suck!'" (Luke 23:29). *Hail Mary…*

7. "Then, they will begin to say to the mountains, 'Fall on us'; and to the hills, 'Cover us'" (Luke 23:30). *Hail Mary…*

8. "For if they do this when the wood is green, what will happen when it is dry?" (Luke 23:31). *Hail Mary…*

9. And they brought him to the place called Golgotha (which means the place of a skull) (Mark 15:22). *Hail Mary…*

10. And they offered him wine mingled with myrrh; but he did not take it (Mark 15:23). *Hail Mary…*

THE FIFTH SORROWFUL MYSTERY
THE CRUCIFIXION

1. And when they came to the place which is called The Skull, there they crucified him, and the criminals, one on the right and one on the left (Luke 23:33). *Hail Mary...*

2. And Jesus said, "Father, forgive them; for they know not what they do" (Luke 23:34). *Hail Mary...*

3. One of the criminals who were hanged railed at him, saying, "Are you not the Christ? Save yourself and us!" (Luke 23:39). *Hail Mary...*

4. But the other rebuked him.... And he said, "Jesus, remember me when you come in your kingly power" (Luke 23:40, 42). *Hail Mary...*

5. And he said to him, "Truly, I say to you, today you will be with me in Paradise" (Luke 23:43). *Hail Mary...*

6. When Jesus saw his mother, and the disciple whom he loved standing near, he said to his mother, "Woman, behold, your son!" Then he said to the disciple, "Behold, your mother!" (John 19:26–27). *Hail Mary...*

7. And about the ninth hour Jesus cried with a loud voice..."My God, my God, why have you forsaken me?" (Matthew 27:46). *Hail Mary...*

8. After this Jesus, knowing that all was now finished, said (to fulfill the scripture), "I thirst" (John 19:28). *Hail Mary...*

9. So they put a sponge full of the vinegar on hyssop and held it to his mouth. When Jesus had received the vinegar, he said, "It is finished" (John 19:29–30). *Hail Mary...*

10. Then Jesus, crying with a loud voice, said, "Father, into your hands I commit my spirit!" And having said this he breathed his last (Luke 23:46). *Hail Mary...*

THE FIRST GLORIOUS MYSTERY
THE RESURRECTION

1. Now after the sabbath, toward the dawn of the first day of the week, Mary Magdalene and the other Mary went to see the tomb (Matthew 28:1). *Hail Mary...*

2. And they found the stone rolled away from the tomb, but when they went in they did not find the body (Luke 24:2–3). *Hail Mary...*

3. While they were perplexed about this, behold, two men stood by them in dazzling apparel; the men said to them, "Why do you seek the living among the dead? He is not here, but has risen" (Luke 24:4–5). *Hail Mary...*

4. So they departed quickly from the tomb with fear and great joy, and ran to tell his disciples (Matthew 28:8). *Hail Mary...*

5. And behold, Jesus met them and said, "Hail!" And they came up and took hold of his feet and worshiped him (Matthew 28:9). *Hail Mary...*

6. On the evening of that day...the doors being shut where the disciples were, for fear of the Jews, Jesus came and stood among them and said to them, "Peace be with you" (John 20:19). *Hail Mary...*

7. When he had said this, he showed them his hands and his side (John 20:20). *Hail Mary...*

8. [Jesus] said to Thomas, "Put your finger here, and see my hands; and put out your hand, and place it in my side; do not be faithless, but believing" (John 20:27). *Hail Mary...*

9. Thomas answered him, "My Lord and my God!" (John 20:28). *Hail Mary...*

10. Jesus said to him, "You have believed because you have seen me. Blessed are those who have not seen and yet believe" (John 20:29). *Hail Mary...*

THE SECOND GLORIOUS MYSTERY
THE ASCENSION

1. To them [Jesus] presented himself alive after his passion by many proofs, appearing to them during forty days, and speaking of the kingdom of God (Acts 1:3). *Hail Mary…*

2. So when they had come together, they asked him, "Lord, will you at this time restore the kingdom to Israel?" (Acts 1:6). *Hail Mary…*

3. He said to them, "It is not for you to know times or seasons which the Father has fixed by his own authority" (Acts 1:7). *Hail Mary…*

4. "But you shall receive power when the Holy Spirit has come upon you" (Acts 1:8). *Hail Mary…*

5. "And you shall be my witnesses in Jerusalem and in all Judea and Samaria and to the end of the earth" (Acts 1:8). *Hail Mary…*

6. And when he had said this, as they were looking on, he was lifted up, and a cloud took him out of their sight (Acts 1:9). *Hail Mary…*

7. So then the Lord Jesus, after he had spoken to them, was taken up into heaven, and sat down at the right hand of God (Mark 16:19). *Hail Mary…*

8. And while they were gazing into heaven as he went, behold, two men stood by them in white robes (Acts 1:10). *Hail Mary…*

9. [The two men] said, "Men of Galilee, why do you stand looking into heaven?" (Acts 2:11). *Hail Mary…*

10. "This Jesus, who was taken up from you into heaven, will come in the same way as you saw him go into heaven" (Acts 2:11). *Hail Mary…*

THE THIRD GLORIOUS MYSTERY
THE DESCENT OF THE HOLY SPIRIT

1. When the day of Pentecost had come, they were all together in one place (Acts 2:1). *Hail Mary...*

2. And suddenly a sound came from heaven like the rush of a mighty wind, and it filled all the house where they were sitting (Acts 2:2). *Hail Mary...*

3. And there appeared to them tongues as of fire, distributed and resting on each one of them (Acts 2:3). *Hail Mary...*

4. And they were all filled with the Holy Spirit and began to speak in other tongues, as the Spirit gave them utterance (Acts 2:4). *Hail Mary...*

5. Now there were dwelling in Jerusalem Jews, devout men from every nation under heaven. And at this sound the multitude came together, and they were bewildered, because each one heard them speaking in his own language (Acts 2:5–6). *Hail Mary...*

6. But Peter, standing with the eleven, lifted up his voice and addressed them, "Men of Judea and all who dwell in Jerusalem...this is what was spoken by the prophet Joel" (Acts 2:14, 16). *Hail Mary...*

7. "And in the last days it shall be, God declares, that I will pour out my Spirit upon all flesh, and your sons and your daughters shall prophesy" (Acts 2:17; see Joel 2:28). *Hail Mary...*

8. "Let all the house of Israel therefore know assuredly that God has made him both Lord and Christ, this Jesus whom you crucified" (Acts 2:36). *Hail Mary...*

9. And Peter said to them, "Repent, and be baptized every one of you in the name of Jesus Christ for the forgiveness of your sins; and you shall receive the gift of the Holy Spirit" (Acts 2:38). *Hail Mary...*

10. So those who received his word were baptized, and there were added that day about three thousand souls (Acts 2:41). *Hail Mary…*

THE FOURTH GLORIOUS MYSTERY
THE ASSUMPTION OF MARY

1. "Arise, my love, my dove, my fair one, and come away" (Song 2:10). *Hail Mary…*

2. "You are all fair, my love; there is no flaw in you" (Song 4:7). *Hail Mary…*

3. Arise, O Lord, and go to your resting place, you and the ark of your might (Psalm 132:8). *Hail Mary…*

4. Then God's temple in heaven was opened, and the ark of his covenant was seen within his temple (Revelation 11:19). *Hail Mary…*

5. And a great sign appeared in heaven, a woman clothed with the sun (Revelation 12:1). *Hail Mary…*

6. "Who is this that looks forth like the dawn, fair as the moon, bright as the sun?" (Song 6:10). *Hail Mary…*

7. "Hail, full of grace, the Lord is with you!" (Luke 1:28). *Hail Mary…*

8. "Blessed are you among women" (Luke 1:42). *Hail Mary…*

9. "For behold, henceforth all generations will call me blessed; for he who is mighty has done great things for me" (Luke 1:48–49). *Hail Mary…*

10. "You are the exaltation of Jerusalem, you are the great glory of Israel, you are the great pride of our nation!" (Judith 15:9). *Hail Mary…*

THE FIFTH GLORIOUS MYSTERY
THE CROWNING OF MARY

1. So Bathsheba went to King Solomon…and the king rose to meet her, and bowed down to her (1 Kings 2:19). *Hail Mary…*

2. Then he sat on his throne, and had a seat brought for the king's mother; and she sat on his right (1 Kings 2:19). *Hail Mary...*

3. Then she said, "I have one small request to make of you; do not refuse me" (1 Kings 2:20). *Hail Mary...*

4. And the king said to her, "Make your request, my mother; for I will not refuse you" (1 Kings 2:20). *Hail Mary...*

5. [The angel said to Mary,] "And behold, you will conceive in your womb and bear a son...and the Lord God will give to him the throne of his father David" (Luke 1:31–32). *Hail Mary...*

6. [Elizabeth said to Mary,] "And why is this granted me, that the mother of my Lord should come to me?" (Luke 1:43). *Hail Mary...*

7. And a great sign appeared in heaven, a woman clothed with the sun, with the moon under her feet (Revelation 12:1). *Hail Mary...*

8. And on her head [was] a crown of twelve stars (Revelation 12:1). *Hail Mary...*

9. She brought forth a male child, one who is to rule all the nations with a rod of iron (Revelation 12:5). *Hail Mary...*

10. But her child was caught up to God and to his throne (Revelation 12:5). *Hail Mary...*

PREFACE

1. Quotes from Pope John Paul II's Apostolic Letter on the Most Holy Rosary, *Rosarium Virginis Mariae* (indicated as *RVM*), October 16, 2002, are from the Vatican website, https://w2.vatican.va/content/john-paul-ii/en/apost_letters/2002/documents/hf_jp-ii_apl_20021016_rosarium-virginis-mariae.html.

CHAPTER ONE

1. St. Catherine of Siena, *The Dialogue* (New York: Paulist Press, 1980), p. 42.

CHAPTER TWO

1. Cardinal Joseph Ratzinger, *God and the World* (San Francisco: Ignatius, 2002), p. 320.

2. St. Thomas Aquinas, *Summa Theologiae*, art. 13, www.newadvent.org/summa/1013.htm.

3. St. Thérèse of Lisieux, *Story of a Soul*, trans. Fr. John Clarke, O.C.D. (Washington, D.C.: ICS, 2002), p. 199.

CHAPTER THREE

1. The reason any of our prayers are efficacious is that we pray in the name of Jesus Christ. All prayerful intercession takes place through the mediation of the one mediator, Christ. Thus, the fact that we can pray for each other as Christians actually manifests even more brilliantly the power of Christ's mediation. The same is true with Mary's intercession for us. As the *Catechism of the Catholic Church* (*CCC*) explains: "Mary's function...in no way obscures or diminishes this unique mediation of Christ, but rather shows its power. But the Blessed Virgin's salutary influence on men...flows forth from the superabundance of the merits of Christ, rests on his mediation, depends entirely on it, and draws all its power from it" (*CCC*, 970).

CHAPTER FIVE

1. Robert Barron, *The Strangest Way: Walking the Christian Path* (New York: Orbis, 2002), p. 56.

CHAPTER SEVEN

1. Pope Paul VI, *Marialis Cultus*, Apostolic Exhortation for the Right Ordering of Devotion to the Blessed Virgin Mary, no. 47, February 2, 1974.

2. Barron, p. 55.

3. The repetition of the Hail Mary is meant to serve this purpose. Since the Hail Mary is a biblical prayer centered on Christ, it is fitting that the mysteries of salvation pass before the eyes of the soul against the backdrop of this prayer. As Pope Paul VI once said, "As a Gospel prayer, centered on the mystery of the redemptive

Incarnation, the Rosary is therefore a prayer with a clearly Christological orientation. Its most characteristic element, in fact, the litany-like succession of Hail Marys, becomes in itself an unceasing praise of Christ, who is the ultimate object both of the angel's announcement and the greeting of the mother of John the Baptist: 'Blessed is the fruit of your womb'" (Luke 1:42). *Marialis Cultus*, 46.

CHAPTER EIGHT

1. Pope John Paul II, General Audience of May 8, 1996, in John Paul II, *Theotókos: Woman, Mother, Disciple* (Boston: Pauline, 2000), p. 88; also see *Redemptoris Mater* (indicated as *RM*), Encyclical on the Blessed Virgin Mary in the Life of the Pilgrim Church, 8, March 25, 1987.

2. *RM*, 10.

3. Pope John Paul II, General Audience of September 4, 1996, in *Theotókos*, pp. 134–135.

4. *RM*, 36.

5. Pope John Paul II, General Audience of November 20, 1996, in *Theotókos*, pp. 145–147.

6. See Scott Hahn and Curtis Mitch, *Ignatius Catholic Study Bible: The Gospel of Luke* (San Francisco: Ignatius, 2001), at Luke 2:7.

7. *RM*, 16.

8. *RM*, 18.

9. Romano Guardini, *The Rosary of Our Lady* (Manchester, N.H.: Sophia, 1994), pp. 94–95.

10. Pope John Paul II, Inauguration Homily, October 22, 1978, 5, https:// w2.vatican.va/content/john-paul-ii/en/homilies/1978/documents/hf_jp-ii_ hom_19781022_inizio-pontificato.html.

CHAPTER NINE

1. St. Thomas Aquinas, *Commentary on the Gospel of St. John* (Albany, N.Y.: Magi, 1980), p. 152.

2. *RM*, 21.

3. St. Irenaeus, *Against the Heresies* II, 22, 4, J. Saward, trans., quoted in Hans Urs von Balthasar, ed., *The Scandal of the Incarnation* (San Francisco: Ignatius, 1990), p. 61.

4. John Paul II, General Audience of February 26, 1997, in *Theotókos*, p. 175.

5. St. Bernard of Clairvaux, *On the Song of Songs*, Sermon 36:6, in Kilian Walsh, trans., *On the Song of Songs II* (Kalamazoo, Mich.: Cistercian, 1976), p. 179.

6. Byzantine Liturgy, Feast of the Transfiguration, *Kontakion*. As cited in *CCC*, 555.

CHAPTER TEN

1. See Raymond E. Brown, *Death of the Messiah* (New York: Doubleday, 1994), p. 189.

2. Brown, *Death of the Messiah*, p. 866.

3. N.T. Wright, *Jesus and the Victory of God* (Minneapolis: Fortress, 1996), p. 568.

4. Cicero, "In Defense of Rabirius," 16, in *The Speeches of Cicero*, trans. H. Hodge (Cambridge, Mass.: Harvard, 1952), p. 467.

5. *RM*, 23, quoting John 19:26 and *Lumen Gentium*, 54, 53, which quotes St. Augustine, *De Sancta Virginitate*, VI, 6: PL 40, 399.

CHAPTER ELEVEN

1. See Barron, p. 96.

2. Philo, *On the Decalogue*, 46, in C.D. Yonge, trans., *The Works of Philo* (Peabody, Mass.: Hendrickson, 1993), p. 522. See also L. Johnson, *The Acts of the Apostles* (Collegeville, Minn.: Liturgical Press, 1992), p. 46.

3. See Raymond E. Brown, *An Introduction to the New Testament* (New York: Doubleday, 1997), pp. 283-284; L. Johnson, pp. 45–46; S. Pimentel, *Witness of the Messiah* (Steubenville, Ohio: Emmaus Road, 2002), pp. 29–30.

4. Vatican Council II, Dogmatic Constitution on the Church (*Lumen Gentium*), 59.

5. Pope John Paul II, General Audience of May 28, 1997, in *Theotókos*, pp. 1.

6. Ignace De La Potterie, *Mary in the Mystery of the Covenant* (New York: Alba House, 1992), pp. 17–20. While this passage might point in the direction of the Immaculate Conception, it does not by itself prove it, for Gabriel does not say, "Hail, you who have been graced since the moment of your conception." He simply says, "Hail, graced one," or even more literally, "Hail, you who have been and are now graced."

7. Pope John Paul II, General Audience of June 25, 1997, in *Theotókos*, p. 201.

8. See Pope Pius XII, *Munificentissimus Deus*, as translated in Benedictine Monks of Solesmes, ed., *Our Lady* (Boston: St. Paul Editions, 1961).

9. Pius XII, no. 26.

10. St. Francis de Sales, "Sermon for the Feast of the Assumption," as cited in Pius XII, 35.

11. "The fact that Solomon denies the request in no way discredits the influence of the Gebirah [the queen mother]. Adonijah wanted Abishag the Shunammite for the treacherous purpose of taking over the kingdom from Solomon. (Taking the king's concubine was a sign of usurping the throne in the ancient Near East. For example, see how Absalom, in his attempt to take the throne from David, took his concubines [2 Samuel 16:20-23].) Thus the wickedness of Adonijah's intention is the reason for denial, which in no way reflects negatively upon the Gebirah's power

to intercede. The narrative bears out the fact that the king normally accepted the Gebirah's request. Thus, Solomon says, 'Ask, I will not refuse you.' To say then that this illustrates the weakness of the Gebirah's ability to intercede would be to miss the whole point of the narrative, which tells how Adonijah uses the queen mother's position in an attempt to become king." T. Gray, "God's Word and Mary's Royal Office," *Miles Immaculatae*, 13 (1995), 381, n. 16.

12. My note in "Treat Her Like a Queen," in Leon Suprenant, ed., *Catholic for a Reason II* (Steubenville, Ohio: Emmaus Road, 2000), p. 94, no. 7: "Although the identification of Mary as the 'woman' of Revelation may seem self-evident, some have interpreted this woman as merely a symbol either for the Old Testament People of Israel or for the New Testament Church. They conclude that the woman is not an individual (i.e., Mary), but only a symbol for God's people. However, this 'either-or' proposition is foreign to the Biblical worldview in which individuals often symbolically represent collective groups (e.g., Adam represented all humanity—Romans 5:19; Jacob stood for all of Israel—Psalm 44:4). Given this Biblical notion called 'corporate personality,' the woman in Revelation 12 should be understood as *both* an individual (Mary) *and* a symbol for the People of God. Finally, since the other two main characters in this vision are generally recognized primarily as individuals (the child = Jesus; the dragon = the devil), it seems quite unlikely that the third main character, the woman, is not an individual but only a symbol for a corporate group. Rather, recognizing the woman as Mary makes the most sense out of the text and at the same time is open to viewing her…as a symbol for Israel or the Church."

13. Pope John Paul II, General Audience of July 23, 1997, in *Theotókos*, pp. 211–212.

How to Pray the Rosary

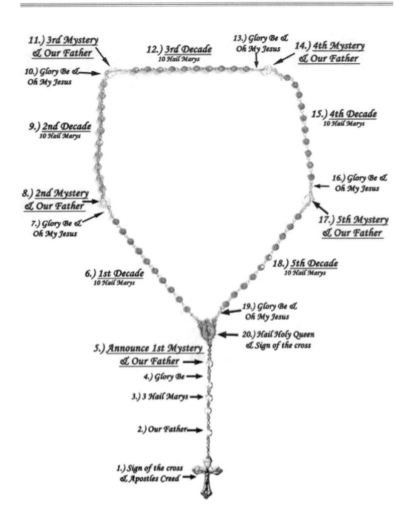

11.) 3rd Mystery & Our Father

12.) 3rd Decade
10 Hail Marys

13.) Glory Be & Oh My Jesus

14.) 4th Mystery & Our Father

10.) Glory Be & Oh My Jesus

15.) 4th Decade
10 Hail Marys

9.) 2nd Decade
10 Hail Marys

16.) Glory Be & Oh My Jesus

8.) 2nd Mystery & Our Father

7.) Glory Be & Oh My Jesus

17.) 5th Mystery & Our Father

6.) 1st Decade
10 Hail Marys

18.) 5th Decade
10 Hail Marys

19.) Glory Be & Oh My Jesus

20.) Hail Holy Queen & Sign of the cross

5.) Announce 1st Mystery & Our Father

4.) Glory Be

3.) 3 Hail Marys

2.) Our Father

1.) Sign of the cross & Apostles Creed

I would like to thank the many people who offered their prayers and encouragement for this project, especially my colleagues and students at the Augustine Institute, Benedictine College and FOCUS (Fellowship of Catholic University Students). I am particularly grateful to Bert Ghezzi, who first suggested that I write a book on the rosary, and to Heidi Saxon for encouraging me to develop this new edition. I also am grateful to Curtis Mitch for his feedback on the original work and for my wife Elizabeth for her support throughout the writing of this book. Finally, I thank my children for their participation in the family rosary each night. May Our Lady's intercession always guide, protect, and strengthen you and may she lead you ever closer to her Son both "now and at the hour of our death."

Dr. Edward Sri is a theologian, author and well-known Catholic speaker who appears regularly on EWTN. Each year he speaks to clergy, parish leaders, catechists and laity from around the world.

He has written several bestselling books, including *Men, Women and the Mystery of Love; A Biblical Walk through the Mass; Walking with Mary;* and *Who Am I to Judge?—Responding to Relativism with Logic and Love.*

Edward Sri is also the host of the acclaimed film series *Symbolon: The Catholic Faith Explained* and the presenter of several popular faith formation film series, including *A Biblical Walk through the Mass; Mary: A Biblical Walk with the Blessed Mother;* and *Follow Me: Meeting Jesus in the Gospel of John.*

He is a founding leader with Curtis Martin of FOCUS (Fellowship of Catholic University Students) and currently serves as a professor of theology at the Augustine Institute in Denver, Colorado.

Dr. Sri leads pilgrimages to Rome and the Holy Land each year. He holds a doctorate from the Pontifical University of St. Thomas Aquinas in Rome. He resides with his wife, Elizabeth, and their eight children in Littleton, Colorado.

You can connect with Edward Sri through his website, www.edwardsri.com, or follow him on Facebook and Twitter.